2nd Edition

Empowering Games & Activities
That Build Resilience in Children

By
Kathy Cooper, M.S.W.
and
Marianne Vandawalker, M.Ed.

YouthLight, Inc.

P.O. Box 115 • Chapin, SC • 29036
(803) 345-1070 • (800) 209-9774
Fax (803) 345-0888 • Email YLDR1@aol.com

Cover Illustrations by Eric Hinson & Elizabeth Madden
Layout & Design by Elizabeth Madden

ISBN 1-889636-01-0
Library of Congress Catalog Card Number 96-061289

9 8 7 6 5 4 3 2 1
Printed in the United States of America

Dedications

To my wonderful husband Bill, for all of his love,
encouragement, and support.

Kathy Cooper

To my husband Larry, who daily cares for me and
the goals that I care about in helping others.

Marianne Vandawalker

Acknowledgements

Throughout the years, I have been fortunate to be in the company of many people who are truly outstanding in the way they love, care, and support me. These people are my friends and I've come to love and appreciate them for all the special gifts they bring. Although these friends are very special, I cannot acknowledge everyone without leaving someone out. However, there are a few that command my highest respect and thanks. I first acknowledge God as the most important Person in my life and the inspiration for all creative ideas. To my mom and dad, for the sacrifices and support they've given throughout the years. To Herb and Virginia for the wonderful parents-in-laws and friends they've become. To Carolyn White and Union County Elementary Counselors for being so caring and supportive. To my fifth grade teacher Bea Colson for pushing me to be creative. Finally, to Benton Heights School for giving me the opportunity to grow and develop and try all of these games and activities with the wonderful children.

Kathy Cooper

I would like to acknowledge my supervisor, Carolyn White, my principal, Dr. Jerry Cross, at Western Union Elementary School and the encouraging teachers and students at that school. The counselors of Union County have also been very supportive.

Also, recognition needs to go to a very wonderful professor, Dr. Wanda Webb, at Davidson College who provided the educational background for the game activities.

Marianne Vandawalker

TABLE OF CONTENTS

PURPOSE 1

SECTION I: CONFLICT RESOLUTION 3

No Fighting! 4

Cooperation 12

Stop It 14

Calm Down 19

Clowning Around 23

Sunshine Game 34

The Ugly Duckling 36

Monster Game 42

Deflate the Balloon 44

The Mean Old Troll 47

Rocky 54

Stone Face 56

Football 58

SECTION II: DECISION MAKING 74

Red Flag 75

The Three Bears 81

Take a Stand 88

Going for the Goal 94

Solving Problems Baseball Game 98

Career Ladder 104

SECTION III: SOCIAL SKILLS 119

Line It Up 120

Who Do You Think You're Talking To? 125

Yes or No Game 136

Catch a Carp (Game one) 149

Catch a Carp (Game two) 150

Millionaire Messages 162

Manners Matter 168

Soap It 176

Attitude Tune Up 179

What If? 185

Take Five 193

Section IV: Cooperation 197

Wahwahlanawah 198

WORDLES™ 201

Balloon Bop 203

Section V: Character Building 205

Mirror, Mirror on the Wall 206

Dress Up, Dress Down 212

Character Parade 218

Who Am I? 223

Wise Man, Foolish Man 228

Pot of Gold 236

Cover It 238

Nasty Noodle 241

Shoot the Hoop 247

Media Mush 249

Operation 252

Section VI: Friendship 261

Stick Together 262

Snowman 269

Friendship Bridge 275

Friendly Flip Out 277

Friendship Follies 287

Hopscotch Happenings 290

SECTION VII: SELF-ESTEEM 295

Jenga® Jive 296
If You're Happy 298
Crater Cross 300
Close Encounters 302
Talking Behind Your Back 304
Duck, Duck, Friend 306
I Can Do It! 308
Musical Dress Up 310
Musical Moves 312
Magazine Madness Scavenger Hunt 314
Look at the Stars 318
The Little Engine That Could 321

SECTION VIII: FEELINGS 325

Upside Down Frown 326
Empty The Stocking 332
Take a Walk 341

SECTION IX: ATTENTION DEFICIT DISORDERS 345

Mind Your Own Business 346
One Track Mind 350
Beat The Clock 352
Attention Circles 354
Center Time 358
Wait A Minute 360
Buddy System 367
The Circle Challenge 369

SECTION X: SAFETY 371

The Three Little Pigs 372
The Gingerbread Man 375

ADDITIONAL RESOURCES 390

POWER ☀ PLAY

PURPOSE

School isn't just about learning how to do math and science anymore. School involves learning how to deal with friends and difficult situations. Unfortunately, there is no magic formula for making any of these situations go away. However, there are strategies and skills that can assist students in many difficult situations.

Power Play is designed to empower students to deal with their problems in a positive and assertive manner. The book is designed to help children become responsible, face their problems, and become more independent while dealing with antagonistic students. The games and activities also teach friendship-making skills and appropriate ways of interacting with other children. The games and activities described in *Power Play* are presented in a non-threatening manner to encourage greater participation from a broader range of students.

Using activities from *Power Play*, students are encouraged to learn various skills through a game format. Activities can be used in a variety of settings such as whole class guidance lessons, small group counseling sessions, or individual counseling sessions. Counselors must be prepared to help students in different situations using a variety of interventions, and *Power Play* provides a creative approach for learning to deal with difficult situations while providing an opportunity for fun and laughter at the same time. Utilizing a fast-paced presentation style, the activities are simple and direct approaches to dealing with uncomfortable encounters. The games require few props and are relatively simple to prepare. Most games steer clear of a lot of paper and pencil activities to allow active participation of all students in a non-threatening manner.

A game format is useful in teaching guidance and counseling for many reasons:

1. Games are less intimidating and threatening to students than openly discussing feelings in a classroom situation.

2. Games provide a higher level of student participation and involvement which helps in class management.

3. Games are fun, positive, and thought provoking.

4. Games require different learning styles including auditory, visual, and kinesthetic.

5. Games provide role-playing and modeling opportunities.

6. Games enhance memory through participation, and they serve as points of reference to remind students of various lessons learned.

7. Games can be enjoyed again and again for added proficiency in skills.

8. Games allow positive behaviors to be immediately reinforced with points, rewards, treats, or applause.

9. Games simulate life situations by calling for quick thinking and quick responses.

10. Game concepts and solutions are reality-based and provide opportunities for cognitive restructuring for therapeutic purposes.

11. Games provide an opportunity for overlearning concepts by emphasizing similar skills in a variety of activities.

12. Games provide an enjoyable format for children to learn; usually children are very receptive to concepts presented in this manner.

The games in this book also contain a most important section - the follow-up section. This section includes questions to be discussed after each game is played. These questions allow students to more fully understand how the skills learned can be used in the classroom, on the playground, in the cafeteria, or in other situations around the school. Questions and answers offer encouragement and support for students to try the techniques in situations similar to those in the games.

Variations are included for easy adaptation to the needs of the students. Since the games provided grow out of real-life circumstances, the situation and response cards must be continually updated for relevancy to student needs.

In essence, the activities are designed to boost self-assurance, self-confidence, and enhance a student's self-image. *Power Play* encourages students to become assertive and independent to solve their problems. Consequently, students are equipped with a variety of strategies to help them deal with problematic social situations. These strategies enable students to enter adolescence and young adulthood with strong social skills, confidence, and effective methods of dealing with problems, which will help them deal with conflict effectively, develop positive character traits, and become responsible citizens.

Section I:

Many times, discord among elementary students begins with a small occurrence such as a look, a nudge, or an inappropriate phrase. If these occurrences aren't dealt with, even the smallest incident can skyrocket into a more threatening situation. Therefore, most of these situations need to be handled immediately by the students involved. Students need to feel confident that they are able to handle these situations without always running to an adult. Hence the need for teaching children strategies to deal with conflict as it arises.

The conflict resolution games and activities in this section reflect many situations that children deal with daily and offer a variety of strategies to use to confront these situations. Children will learn how to be assertive, use humor, change the subject, use comebacks, and use agreement to deal with their problems themselves. These strategies are taught in a fun manner and children may choose the ones they like the best and incorporate them into their own style. Through the use of conflict resolution strategies, children will become confident dealing with problematic situations and enjoy learning methods to help them as they encounter a variety of problems.

CONFLICT

Resolution

No Fighting!

Grade Levels: 2-5

Time: 30 Minutes

PURPOSE

To teach students appropriate social skills for dealing with problems in the classroom.

MATERIALS NEEDED

No Fighting! Situation Cards
(reproduced & cutout)
Chalkboard
Timer

OBJECT

To get points by answering question on situation cards and placing your teams name on the board.

PROCEDURES

1. Place situation cards in a stack. The cards reflect various social situations students face.

2. Assign point values to cards based on the difficulty of the questions. Points can range from one to three. Note: If you have a large game board, use this point system. If you have a small game board, assign all cards a point value of one.

3. On the black board, write the words NO FIGHTING, draw 10 or more rows of blocks under each letter and number all the boxes down the side. See diagram on page 5.

4. Divide the children into teams of four. Give each group a title or allow the children to think of a name for their group.

N	O	F	I	G	H	T	I	N	G

5. Allow the first team to choose up to six cards from the situation card stack. The other teams will choose cards during their turns.

6. Use a timer to give each team a specific time frame to solve the problems listed on each card.

7. Start the timer, then randomly choose a card from the six previously chosen by the team (see #5) and read the question. Determine if the response is appropriate. An appropriate response is one that is not aggressive toward the other students and would appear to address the situation adequately. If the students cannot think of an answer, do not give hints, but go onto another card. If the answer is correct, move onto another question.

8. Add the number of points garnered, and announce the total for the round. The team is then asked to place their name in a corresponding number of boxes on the game board. For instance, if the teams earned six points, then they are asked to write their team's name in any six boxes on the board.

9. Play continues until all groups have played and the boxes on the board have been filled. It is important to make sure all teams have a turn.

10. There must be an adequate number of boxes on the board to accommodate the point values on the cards. If you think this might be a problem, you may forego the point system and award one point for each question answered.

11. After all teams have played and all boxes on the board are filled, the leader of the activity turns his/her back on the game board and randomly chooses a letter and a number. The letters are one of the NO FIGHTING letters and the numbers are those to the left of the game board. For example, N 9 or H 5 may be chosen as the winning groups. The students are instructed that only one group will be chosen as a winner and prizes are awarded to this group. If no prizes are to be given, the team that has claimed the highest number of boxes wins.

VARIATIONS

1. Other phrases can be substituted for "No Fighting" on the board, such as "No Tattling," "Homework," "On-task," etc. The leader would write this word or words on the board and draw blocks underneath the letters as previously described.

2. Instead of playing the game with question cards, you can reward students by asking them to place their initials in blocks for doing or not doing a particular predetermined behavior. For example, someone who did not tattle could put their name in a "No Tattling" block, etc. At the end of the week or day, prizes could randomly be awarded.

FOLLOW-UP

Focus discussion on the various problem-solving strategies and/or solutions students learned while playing the game. You can reinforce these ideas by having a blank game board on the blackboard at all times. Whenever a student uses one of these strategies, the student would place their name in one of the blocks, and you could reward the students at the end of the week by random selection.

SITUATION CARDS FOR NO FIGHTING

No Fighting Cards

SOMEONE IS TAPPING
ON YOUR BACK.
WHAT DO YOU DO?

No Fighting Cards

SOMEONE SAYS THEY'LL
BEAT YOU UP
IN THE BATHROOM.
WHAT DO YOU DO?

No Fighting Cards

SOMEONE IS TRYING TO
GET YOU TO FIGHT.
WHAT DO YOU DO?

No Fighting Cards

SOMEONE IS MAKING FUN
OF YOUR FAMILY.
WHAT DO YOU DO?

No Fighting Cards

SOMEONE HAS A
KNIFE AT SCHOOL.
WHAT DO YOU DO?

No Fighting Cards

SOMEONE SAYS IF YOU
DON'T DO WHAT
THEY SAY, THEY'LL BEAT YOU UP.
WHAT DO YOU DO?

No Fighting Cards

SOMEONE IS TALKING BADLY
ABOUT YOUR GRANDMOTHER.
WHAT DO YOU DO?

No Fighting Cards

SOMEONE PURPOSEFULLY
KNOCKS OVER YOUR
MILK AT LUNCH.
WHAT DO YOU DO?

8

No Fighting Cards

SOMEONE SAYS YOUR
MOTHER IS A FAT PIG.
WHAT DO YOU DO?

No Fighting Cards

SOMEONE CALLS YOU
A NERD.
WHAT DO YOU DO?

No Fighting Cards

SOMEONE IS TALKING
BADLY ABOUT
YOU TO YOUR FRIENDS.
WHAT DO YOU DO?

No Fighting Cards

SOMEONE BREAKS IN
FRONT OF YOU IN LINE.
WHAT DO YOU DO?

No Fighting Cards

SOMEONE CALLS YOU STUPID.
WHAT DO YOU DO?

No Fighting Cards

SOMEONE STEALS THE
KICKBALL FROM YOU.
WHAT DO YOU DO?

No Fighting Cards

SOMEONE KEEPS PLAYING WITH
YOUR HAIR. YOU
DON'T LIKE IT.
WHAT DO YOU DO?

No Fighting Cards

SOMEONE CALLS YOU A NAME.
WHAT DO YOU DO?

No Fighting Cards

SOMEONE PUSHES YOU WHEN YOU'RE IN LINE.
WHAT DO YOU DO?

No Fighting Cards

SOMEONE PUSHES YOU OFF THE SWING.
WHAT DO YOU DO?

No Fighting Cards

SOMEONE TAKES YOUR PENCIL.
WHAT DO YOU DO?

No Fighting Cards

SOMEONE IS HITTING YOUR FRIEND.
WHAT DO YOU DO?

No Fighting Cards

SOMEONE TRIPS YOU ON THE PLAYGROUND.
WHAT DO YOU DO?

No Fighting Cards

SOMEONE SAYS THEY'LL BEAT YOU UP ON THE PLAYGROUND.
WHAT DO YOU DO?

No Fighting Cards

SOMEONE IS ROLLING THEIR EYES AT YOU.
WHAT DO YOU DO?

No Fighting Cards

SOMEONE IS TRYING TO COPY YOUR WORK.
WHAT DO YOU DO?

No Fighting Cards

SOMEONE PINCHES YOUR ARM. WHAT DO YOU DO?

No Fighting Cards

SOMEONE CALLS YOUR FRIEND A NERD. WHAT DO YOU DO?

No Fighting Cards

SOMEONE SNATCHES YOUR PAPER. WHAT DO YOU DO?

No Fighting Cards

SOMEONE HITS YOU ON THE BACK. WHAT DO YOU DO?

No Fighting Cards

SOMEONE SAYS YOU KISSED A BOY OR GIRL. YOU DIDN'T. WHAT DO YOU DO?

No Fighting Cards

SOMEONE STEPS ON YOUR FOOT. WHAT DO YOU DO?

No Fighting Cards

YOUR FRIEND WON'T SPEAK TO YOU. WHAT DO YOU DO?

No Fighting Cards

SOMEONE TAKES YOUR BOOK. WHAT DO YOU DO?

No Fighting Cards

SOMEONE SAYS YOUR CLOTHES ARE CHEAP. WHAT DO YOU DO?

No Fighting Cards

SOMEONE CALLS YOU A DUMMY. WHAT DO YOU DO?

No Fighting Cards

SOMEONE CALLS YOU A CHICKEN FOR WALKING AWAY. WHAT DO YOU DO?

No Fighting Cards

SOMEONE TELLS A LIE ABOUT YOU! WHAT DO YOU DO?

No Fighting Cards

SOMEONE TELLS YOU THAT THEY WON'T PLAY WITH YOU ANYMORE. WHAT DO YOU DO?

No Fighting Cards

SOMEONE KEEPS PUSHING AND KICKING WHEN THE TEACHER ISN'T WATCHING IN THE LINE. WHAT DO YOU DO?

No Fighting Cards

SOMEONE LAUGHS AT YOUR ART PICTURE. WHAT DO YOU DO?

No Fighting Cards

SOMEONE TELLS A LIE ABOUT YOU! WHAT DO YOU DO?

COOPERATION

Grade Levels: 3-6

Time: 30 Minutes

PURPOSE

To review words and phrases dealing with conflict resolution.

MATERIALS NEEDED

Point Chart
Timer
No Fighting! Situation Cards
(reproduced & cutout)

OBJECTS

To get the highest number of points.
To be the first to reach a certain
number of points (600).

PROCEDURES

1. Divide the group into two teams.

2. Make a chart as shown on page 13, with the following terms and point values:

3. Review the terms listed by presenting questions whose answers represent some of the above terms. The team that guesses the terms correctly can have 25 points. For example:
   a. Someone takes your book. "Please give back my book." (Talking friendly).
   b. Someone talks about your friend. "Did you see that movie on TV last night?" (Changing the subject).

4. Play begins by giving each team turns at answering situation cards. Using the questions given, ask each team to answer as many situation cards as possible in one minute.

Ignore	50	Compliment	50
Walk away	75	Use self talk	100
Talk friendly	100	Make a deal	50
Talk firmly	100	Say how you feel	100
Get an adult to help	25	Negotiate	100
Apologize	25	Consensus	125
Use humor	75	Compromise	125
Ask questions	50	Win Win	125
Change the subject	75	Restitution	150
Vote	75		

Note: Although most point values are arbitrary, those interventions that are more difficult for children are higher.

5. To answer a question correctly, the team must state the conflict resolution phrase written on the chart above and then say the actual way they would respond to the question. For example, one student might say they would "talk friendly" and say, "Please leave me alone." The purpose of this is to assure not only can the student choose a correct response, but also that they can use the response in a specific situation.

6. If you deem the answer appropriate, the team is given the number of points assigned to that conflict resolution phrase. For example, the answer "talk friendly" followed by the appropriate example, would be 100 points.

7. Play continues as time allows.

STOP IT

Grade Levels: 4-5

Time: 30 Minutes

PURPOSE

To teach students a method of confronting
others who are manipulative.

MATERIALS NEEDED

Stop It cards (reproduced & cutout)
Basket

OBJECT

To get the most points by
employing the Stop It method in a
role-playing situation.

PROCEDURES

1. Divide students into two teams.

2. Depending on the age of the students, discuss several kinds of con-games or negative behaviors that students play with each other. Students often use certain manipulating behaviors to get what they want from other people. Some examples are:

    a. Students may act helpless to get out of doing an assignment.

    b. Students may act like bullies to get attention from other people.

    c. Students may do silly things in the classroom to get others to laugh at them.

    d. Students may act sick because it causes their friends to give them sympathy.

    e. Students may lie about what they've done or where they've gone because it causes their friends to think they're in a higher social class.

    f. Students may have temper tantrums because it gets them what they want.

    g. Students may act like the work is too hard because this causes others to help them or give them the answers.

3.   Explain the STOP method (see next page).

4.   Place all Stop It Situation Cards in a basket.

5.   Each student takes a turn picking one of the cards from the basket.

6.   During each student's turn, he/she chooses another student on their team with whom to act out the game.

7.   The student who is receiving the game behavior is asked to use the STOP method. For example, Jane chose the "bully" card and acted it out with Susie. Susie then:
   •   States the behavior: "Jane, you're pushing me around and acting like a bully."
   •   Talks about the desired behavior: "I would like it if you would play catch with me."
   •   Offers a choice: "If you would like to play catch, I will play with you. If not, I will go play with someone else."
   •   Provides the consequence: Jane continued pushing her, so Susie just walked away.

8.   Students are awarded up to four points, one for completing each of the steps in the STOP method.   You determine if the steps have been clearly followed.

FOLLOW-UP

After each role-play, encourage a discussion about other options. Students can talk about appropriate consequences such as walking away, choosing other friends to play with, or getting adult intervention when necessary. Students need to have a variety of strategies available to use against manipulative behaviors.

STOP METHOD

S tate the current manipulative behavior or what the student is actually doing.

T alk to the student about the preferred or desired behavior.

O ffer the student choices.

P rovide a consequence for continued misbehavior.

The model below is a way of dealing with manipulative behavior.

1. State the behavior: "Susan, you are calling me names."

2. Talk to the student about the preferred behavior: "I would like you to stop."

3. Offer choices: "If you stop, I'll play with you at recess. If you don't, I'll play with other friends."

4. Provide a consequence: If Susan keeps on teasing, the student can walk away.

Another Example

1. State the behavior: "Audia, you are pouting."

2. Talk to the student about the preferred behavior: "I would like for you to talk with me about what's wrong."

3. Offer choices: "If you keep pouting, I won't be able to talk with you. If you quit pouting, I would love to help you and talk to you."

4. Provide a consequence: The student would act accordingly and you would either talk with her or move away from her.

Note that if "STOP" doesn't change the unwanted behavior in the other student, there needs to be a backup plan, such as telling a teacher.

STOP IT CARDS

Stop It Cards

Bully
Act tough and try to threaten the other person.

Stop It Cards

Stubborn
Refuse to budge. Tell your friend they will need to do it your way or else you won't play.

Stop It Cards

Whiner
Act as if you never get your way and beg someone to help you do your work.

Stop It Cards

"I Can't"
Act as if you are helpless and can't accomplish a things. Keep saying "I can't" in a pitiful voice.

Stop It Cards

Helpless
Act pitiful and complain about how hard everything is and how you need a lot of help.

Stop It Cards

Fearful
Act as if you are scared of everything- of getting an F, of falling on the playground, of getting a cold, of no one liking you, etc.

Stop It Cards

Cool
Act like you believe you are the coolest, toughest, and most handsome or prettiest in the school.

Stop It Cards

Name Calling
Call your friend stupid, dumb, and ridiculous.

POWER PLAY

Stop It Cards

Temper Tantrum
Act really mad because you can't play with the other person's toys.

STOP

Stop It Cards

Cutesy
Act like a "cute" little girl - primping, being very sweet, prancing around, etc.

STOP

Stop It Cards

Don't Care
Act as if you don't care when your teacher gives you work. It's really too hard, but you don't want to tell her so you act as if you don't care to get out of it.

STOP

Stop It Cards

Blamer
Always blame others. Tell your friend that it's the teacher's fault you aren't doing well, your mom's fault that you have no friends and your best friend's fault that you made an F in math because she didn't help you.

STOP

Stop It Cards

Clowning
Act ridiculous - Jump around, laugh - try to get everyone's attention.

STOP

Stop It Cards

Tear Jerker
Cry every time something is too hard, or when you don't get your way.

STOP

Stop It Cards

Sour Grapes
Act as if you didn't want to do a certain thing because it's no fun anyway.

STOP

Stop It Cards

Pouter
Act as if you're very angry and sad for not getting your way - stick out your lower lip and make a frown.

STOP

POWER PLAY

CALM DOWN

Grade Levels: K-5

Time: 30 Minutes

PURPOSE

To help students to deflate their frustrating, angry feelings that can lead to being out of control.

MATERIALS NEEDED

A small ball or object on a string attached to a small pulley, or an untied balloon

Calm Down Cards (reproduced, cutout & glued to half sheets of construction paper)

Bean bag or other object that can be thrown

OBJECT

To calm down before the ball drops, or the balloon is empty.

PROCEDURES

1. Divide students into two teams.

2. Spread out the Calm Down Cards face down on the floor in a central location.

3. Ask one student to throw the bean bag on a card, pick up the card the bean bag lands on, and read the calm down technique.

4. The student attempts to do the calm down technique while the ball is very slowly lowered to the floor or while the leader slowly lets out all of the air in a balloon.

5. Other students on their team may practice while the one student is meeting the challenge.

VARIATIONS

1. Students can practice calm down techniques described on the cards individually or in small groups.

2. A round of applause, stickers, certificates, etc. may be handed out for achieving a calm down technique.

3. Students can draw a picture of a situation that causes them to be angry, frustrated, to yell, hit or curse. These drawings can remind them of times to use the calm down technique.

FOLLOW-UP

Have the student ask him/herself: "Which calm down technique worked the best for me? In what situations would my favorite technique help me calm down? How would I feel after calming down?"

Calm Down Cards

© 1997 by YouthLight, Inc.

Calm Down Cards

Do jumping jacks

25

Calm Down Cards

Pinch your ear lightly 30 times

50

Calm Down Cards

Take a walk

(back and forth for the game)

25

Calm Down Cards

Take a big breath and slowly let it out

75

Calm Down Cards

Clench your fist

(open and shut 20 times)

25

Calm Down Cards

Put your head down and rest

50

Calm Down Cards

Get a drink of water

75

Calm Down Cards

Hold your arm or leg stiff for a count of 12

100

Calm Down Cards

COUNT DOWN FROM 50

25

Calm Down Cards

COUNT TO 25

50

Calm Down Cards

HUM A FAVORITE SONG TO YOURSELF

75

Calm Down Cards

THINK OF TEN OF YOUR FAVORITE THINGS TO DO

100

Calm Down Cards

PULL YOUR SHOULDERS UP TO YOUR EARS FOR A COUNT OF 12

25

Calm Down Cards

THROW AN IMAGINARY BASEBALL 12 TIMES

50

Calm Down Cards

TIGHTEN YOUR STOMACH MUSCLES FOR A COUNT OF 12

75

Calm Down Cards

HOP ON ONE FOOT 20 TIMES

100

CLOWNING AROUND

Grade Levels: 2-5

Time: 30 Minutes

PURPOSE

To help students learn to respond appropriately to teasing statements.

MATERIALS NEEDED

Clowning Around board
Clowning Around Teasing Cards*
Clowning Around Silly Cards*
One die
Team markers (colored squares or little people)

* reproduced & cutout

OBJECT

To reach the end of the board or to get the most points by responding appropriately.

PROCEDURES

1. Make a game board which has about two thirds blank spaces and one third clowning or silly face spaces or enlarge the game board on page 25. The game board should have a beginning and an end, and be large enough so that most students can see it (you may want to tape it to the wall or board and tape the markers to the board as the teams move).

2. The Clowning Around Teasing Cards have comments that children may say to each other, as well as various point values. The Clowning Around Silly Cards are silly pantomimes children perform. Examples: Bark like a dog, act like you're playing the piano, etc.

3. Teach students various ways of responding to teasing, include the use of humor, agreement with statements, change the subject, compliment, etc. A list of these may be placed on the blackboard for reference, and you may give several examples of each before play begins.

4. Divide the class into two teams. Teams will compete to see who can reach the end first.

5. A student rolls the die. When students land on a blank spot, they pick a Teasing Card to answer. If they land on a silly face, they pick a Clowning Around Silly Card and perform the pantomime until it is their team's turn again. A scorekeeper should keep record of the points acquired from the Teasing Cards.

6. Play continues until one team reaches the end of the game board before the other team. Points are tallied to determine which team received the highest number. Therefore, two teams could possibly win: The team who reaches the end of the board first and the team who accumulates the most points.

FOLLOW-UP

Have a discussion with the class or group about teasing comments and making appropriate responses. Students are encouraged to continue utilizing these skills in their day-to-day interactions with other students.

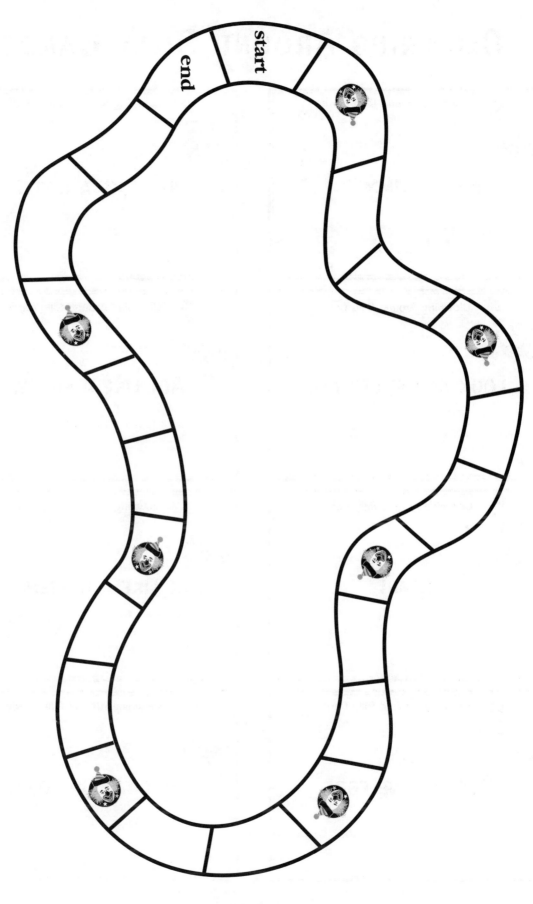

CLOWNING AROUND SILLY CARDS

Clowning Around Silly Cards

BE A SWIMMER.

Clowning Around Silly Cards

ACT LIKE A KITTY.

Clowning Around Silly Cards

LOOK AT THE CEILING.

Clowning Around Silly Cards

ACT LIKE A PUPPY.

Clowning Around Silly Cards

JUMP!

Clowning Around Silly Cards

ACT LIKE A BUTTERFLY.

Clowning Around Silly Cards

HOP ON ONE FOOT.

Clowning Around Silly Cards

TOUCH YOUR TOES.

Clowning Around Silly Cards

ACT LIKE A SNAKE.

 Clowning Around Silly Cards

WALK AROUND
THE ROOM.

 Clowning Around Silly Cards

ACT LIKE A
PIECE OF POPCORN.

 Clowning Around Silly Cards

SHOVEL DIRT.

 Clowning Around Silly Cards

ACT LIKE A TURTLE.

 Clowning Around Silly Cards

ACT LIKE A DUCK.

 Clowning Around Silly Cards

TWIRL.

 Clowning Around Silly Cards

COUNT TO 50.

Clowning Around Silly Cards

DO THE TWIST.

 Clowning Around Silly Cards

TOUCH YOUR NOSE.

 Clowning Around Silly Cards

BLINK!

 Clowning Around Silly Cards

TOUCH YOUR KNEE.

 Clowning Around Silly Cards

HUM!

 Clowning Around Silly Cards

COUGH!

 Clowning Around Silly Cards

DO JUMPING JACKS.

 Clowning Around Silly Cards

YAWN!

Clowning Around Silly Cards

GO TO SLEEP.

Clowning Around Silly Cards

ROLL YOUR HEAD

IN CIRCLES.

Clowning Around Silly Cards

GO LOOK OUT

THE WINDOW.

Clowning Around Silly Cards

LIE ON THE FLOOR.

Clowning Around Silly Cards

SCRATCH YOUR HEAD.

Clowning Around Silly Cards

PAT YOUR HEAD AND

RUB YOUR STOMACH.

Clowning Around Silly Cards

GIVE A BIG LAUGH.

Clowning Around Silly Cards

STOMP ON ANTS.

CLOWNING AROUND TEASING CARDS

Clowning Around Teasing Cards

SOMEONE SAYS YOU HAVE

A BIG NOSE.

25

Clowning Around Teasing Cards

SOMEONE SAYS YOU HAVE

COOTIES.

100

Clowning Around Teasing Cards

SOMEONE CALLS YOU

A SISSY.

50

Clowning Around Teasing Cards

SOMEONE CALLS YOU

A DONKEY.

50

Clowning Around Teasing Cards

SOMEONE CALLS YOU

STUPID.

75

Clowning Around Teasing Cards

SOMEONE CALLS YOU A

LARGE CHARGE HEAD.

150

Clowning Around Teasing Cards

SOME CALLS YOU A FOOL.

100

Clowning Around Teasing Cards

SOMEONE CALLS YOU

BUTTER TEETH.

125

© 1997 by YouthLight, Inc.

Clowning Around Teasing Cards

SOMEONE CALLS YOU UGLY.

25

Clowning Around Teasing Cards

SOMEONE CALLS YOU

A BIG HEAD.

100

Clowning Around Teasing Cards

SOMEONE CALLS YOU

A BUGAR GIRL.

50

Clowning Around Teasing Cards

SOMEONE CALLS YOU

MRS. BUSH.

50

Clowning Around Teasing Cards

SOMEONE CALLS YOU

A BUGAR BOY.

75

Clowning Around Teasing Cards

SOMEONE CALLS YOU

A PEA BRAIN.

75

Clowning Around Teasing Cards

SOME CALLS YOU FATSO.

100

Clowning Around Teasing Cards

SOMEONE CALLS YOU

STUPID IDIOT.

100

32

Clowning Around Teasing Cards

SOMEONE CALLS YOU

A BUGAR EATER.

50

Clowning Around Teasing Cards

SOMEONE CALLS YOU

BIG TAIL.

125

Clowning Around Teasing Cards

SOMEONE CALLS YOU

TOOTHPICK.

75

Clowning Around Teasing Cards

SOMEONE CALLS YOU

A BRAT.

100

Clowning Around Teasing Cards

SOMEONE CALLS YOU

A BIG TWERP.

125

Clowning Around Teasing Cards

SOMEONE SAYS THIS ABOUT YOUR MOTHER: FATTY, FATTY, 2 BY 4, CAN'T GET THROUGH THE BATHROOM DOOR.

150

Clowning Around Teasing Cards

SOME CALLS YOU BIG LIPS.

25

Clowning Around Teasing Cards

SOMEONE SAYS YOUR

MOTHER IS UGLY

125

Clowning Around Teasing Cards

SOMEONE CALLS YOU CHUBBY CHEEKS.

50

Clowning Around Teasing Cards

SOMEONE SAYS: YOUR MOTHER IS SO STUPID THAT WHEN YOU SAID IT WAS CHILLY OUTSIDE, SHE WENT TO GET A BOWL.

150

Clowning Around Teasing Cards

SOMEONE CALLS YOU STUBBY NOSE.

75

Clowning Around Teasing Cards

SOMEONE SAYS: YOUR MOM IS SO DUMB THAT SHE COOKED MINUTE RICE FOR AN HOUR.

150

Clowning Around Teasing Cards

SOMEONE SAYS YOUR HAIR LOOKS LIKE A SCOURING PAD.

25

Clowning Around Teasing Cards

SOMEONE SAYS YOU'RE GOING TO FAIL YOUR GRADE.

50

Clowning Around Teasing Cards

SOMEONE MAKES FUN OF YOUR GLASSES.

75

Clowning Around Teasing Cards

SOMEONE SAYS THAT YOUR FRIENDS DON'T LIKE YOU.

100

SUNSHINE GAME

Grade Levels: K-3

Time: 30 Minutes

PURPOSE

To help students learn appropriate methods of responding to teasing comments.

MATERIALS NEEDED

Sunshine shapes
Sunshine faces
Black trash bags
Timer

OBJECT

To cross the room before the timer expires while making appropriate responses to the cloud.

PROCEDURES

1. Make 15 - 20 sunshine shapes to place on the floor. Place them randomly so that students do not have to step on all of them to get to the other side.

2. Teach students the skill of using various positive statements to turn around negative thoughts. In particular, teach children "I" statements or other turnaround statements. For example, if one child says, "you're ugly," the other child can respond, "I like the way I look." enabling the child to use cognitive restructuring in order to avoid internalizing negative thoughts.

3. Ask two students to participate in the sunshine game show. These students can wear sunshine faces. (Sunshine shapes with a circle cut in the middle large enough to put the face through.)

4.	Ask another student to be a cloud. This student can wear a "cloud outfit" (a trash bag with a hole in the top for their head).

5.	Turn a sand timer over to start the game.

6.	Ask the two students wearing sunshine faces to try to step across the room only on the sunshines one at a time in order to reach the other side before the sand timer runs out. The student wearing the cloud makes up negative statements. (Note: This usually turns out well because the statements really exemplify what children commonly say.) Whenever the children step, the student playing the cloud should give them a teasing comment or a put-down. The student stepping on sunshines must respond with either a positive "I" statement, a humorous remark, or some other turn around statement. Children on sunshines are not allowed to say put-downs or comparison remarks ("I'm smarter than you"), in return. One teasing comment must be given for each step the sunshine student makes.

7.	The two students win if they are able to cross the room before the timer runs out. If the timer is not very long, only one child may be chosen at a time.

FOLLOW-UP

1.	Discuss ways to deal with teasing comments and challenge students to try these strategies during the week. Discussions should center around appropriate responses that do not include put-downs.

2.	Focus discussion on maintaining sunny or positive thoughts even when others want to make our days cloudy. Explain that through using positive self-talk, one can prevent such thoughts from taking root.

THE UGLY DUCKLING

Grade Levels: 1-5

Time: 30 Minutes

PURPOSE

To help students successfully handle teasing or negative statements, and maintain a perspective on their problems.

MATERIALS NEEDED

Ugly Duckling adapted review
Response Cards (reproduced & cutout)
Small sponge ball
Three ducks (on cardboard or poster board that are folded on the bottom so they can stand alone)

OBJECT

To earn points by correctly identifying negative and positive statements, and turn the negative to positive.

PROCEDURES

1. Review the basic story of the Ugly Duckling. Remind students how the duckling was put down by his family, friends, and the people he met. However, the put-downs did not come true because the duckling turned out to be something totally different from what everyone expected, a beautiful swan.

2. Divide the class into two teams.

3. Each team takes turns taking response cards.

4. Cards need to be answered by deciding if they list a negative statement or a positive statement.

5.   If the card lists a negative statement, the student needs to change the wording to make it a positive statement. Five points are scored if the correct answer is given. One point is scored if the student correctly identifies the statement as a negative statement or a positive statement. For example, if the card says , "You're stupid," the student needs to identify the statement as a negative one and change it to a positive statement, such as ,"You're great."

6.   For five extra points, the student takes one shot, using the sponge ball, at the cardboard ducks. Extra points are earned if a duck is knocked down.

7.   The winning team is the one that has accumulated the most points.

FOLLOW-UP

Ask the students the following questions:

● How are negative statements like throwing things at people? (People make negative statements at random, for fun, or to boost their own self-esteem by putting others down.)

● Does it help to give yourself positive statements?

● How could the story of The Ugly Duckling encourage you to look to the future and not focus on immediate negative incidents?

● Is it important to tell yourself positive things?

POWER ✹ PLAY

Adapted Review of the Ugly Duckling

Once upon a time, as you remember, a duckling hatched who looked different from the other ducklings. All the other ducklings were very unkind to him, calling him the Ugly Duckling. Everywhere he went, following his mother and the other ducklings, he had to endure put-downs and taunting laughter from the others along the way. He took this abuse without any retaliation, but the comments he heard made him feel very badly about himself. In fact, he ran away from his family because he felt so unworthy.

After his season for growing was over, he discovered that others around him were again looking at him, but this time, they were looking in admiration. He looked at his reflection in the water and discovered a magnificent swan, just like the ones that he had always admired. Now he wasn't an ugly duckling after all, but a graceful, handsome swan.

UGLY DUCKLING RESPONSE CARDS

Ugly Duckling Response Cards	Ugly Duckling Response Cards
YOU'RE NO GOOD.	I LIKE YOUR PAPER.
Ugly Duckling Response Cards	Ugly Duckling Response Cards
YOU STINK.	THANK YOU FOR YOUR HELP.
Ugly Duckling Response Cards	Ugly Duckling Response Cards
I LIKE YOU.	YOU'RE MY BEST FRIEND.
Ugly Duckling Response Cards	Ugly Duckling Response Cards
GET AWAY FROM ME.	NO ONE WANTS TO PLAY WITH YOU.

40

Ugly Duckling Response Cards

YOU'RE STUPID.

Ugly Duckling Response Cards

YOU'RE FAT.

Ugly Duckling Response Cards

YOUR IDEA IS GOOD.

Ugly Duckling Response Cards

YOU'RE SKINNY.

Ugly Duckling Response Cards

YOU CAN'T RUN FAST.

Ugly Duckling Response Cards

LEAVE ME ALONE.

Ugly Duckling Response Cards

NOBODY CARES WHAT

YOU SAY.

Ugly Duckling Response Cards

YOU LOOK NICE TODAY.

Ugly Duckling Response Cards

IT'S GOOD TO SEE YOU.

Ugly Duckling Response Cards

YOU ARE UGLY.

Ugly Duckling Response Cards

CAN YOU COME OVER TO MY HOUSE?

Ugly Duckling Response Cards

FOUR EYES.

Ugly Duckling Response Cards

STOP BOTHERING ME.

Ugly Duckling Response Cards

FATSO.

Ugly Duckling Response Cards

YOU'RE JUST LIKE YOUR MEAN BROTHER.

Ugly Duckling Response Cards

YOU'RE THE TEACHER'S PET.

MONSTER GAME

Grade Levels: K-3

Time: 30 Minutes

PURPOSE

To teach students to respond to the teasing comments of others.

MATERIALS NEEDED

Cardboard monster outfit

OBJECT

To kick the monster out of the circle using turnaround statements.

PROCEDURES

1. Make a large monster shape out of cardboard. Cut a hole large enough for a student to put his/her face through it to "wear the suit."

2. Have the students sit in a circle on the floor.

3. Ask one student to play the grouchy monster.

4. The grouchy monster's job is to ruin every child's day by stealing their special feelings. Students are told that the way to tell if the monster stole their special feelings is to see if he made them start feeling grouchy too. Explain that grouchy children put other children down, have angry looks on their faces, and even hit other people sometimes. Explain that happy children respond to teasing with turnaround statements, maintain positive feelings about themselves, and have happy looks on their faces.

5. Lead the students in a self-esteem cheer to make sure they have special feelings. Ask the students to hit the floor two times and clap their hands two times to establish the beat. Each time, the students can repeat a different phrase three times. Examples of phrases might include: I am smart, I am special, I am terrific, I help others, etc. The chant can be changed every time.

6. After the cheer, the monster sneaks into the circle and looks for special feelings to steal. The monster does this by saying a put-down statement to one of the students. In advance, the students are told the secret of scaring the monster away: to state a turnaround statement back to the monster. When the monster hears a turnaround statement, he/she runs out of the circle. (For example, the monster says, "You have ugly hair." The child responds, "I like my hair, thank you.").

7. Students in the circle aren't allowed to make put-down or comparison statements ("At least I'm smarter than you.").

8. After the student scares the monster away, the other students are encouraged to clap.

9. Students take turns being the monster.

10. Prior to each new monster entering the circle, a self-esteem cheer is briefly repeated. Students are told that they need to keep repeating more special feelings to themselves.

FOLLOW-UP

Center the discussion around continuing to use these turnaround statements whenever put-downs arise in the classroom or elsewhere. The book <u>Don't Feed the Monster on Tuesday</u> by Adolph Moser, Ed.D., can be used prior to this activity.

DEFLATE THE BALLOON

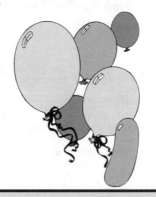

Grade Levels: K-5

Time: 30 Minutes

PURPOSE

To teach students how to express their anger in an appropriate and timely way, before they explode.

MATERIALS NEEDED

BALLOONS

PINS

OBJECT

TO SEE HOW MANY WAYS CAN BE GIVEN TO DEFLATE A POTENTIALLY EXPLOSIVE SITUATION.

PROCEDURES

1. Show the students a deflated balloon. Explain that the balloon is like a person sleeping - nice and relaxed. Choose a student to come up front and act out the person in the story. Explain that each time you blow air into the balloon, it symbolizes the student becoming more angry, anxious, or stressed. Use the student's name and put in any special facts you know about him/her.

2. Begin the story, "The alarm clock just went off, and [name of student] didn't want to get up. Then his/her Mom yells at him/her to 'Hurry up!'" (Quickly puff a little air into the balloon so that it stands up.)

3. Then say, "[name of student] realizes he/she is almost late for school." (Blow a little more into the balloon.)

4. "Next, on his/her way to school, some older students see him/her and make fun of him/her." (Blow a little more into the balloon.)

5. "When [name of student] gets to school, someone knocks his/her books out of his/her hands and his/her papers fall across the floor." (Blow more air into the balloon.)

6. "Next, he/she remembers he/she forgot his/her homework." (More air.)

7. "At lunch, someone spills their milk all over [name of student]'s lunch." (More air.)

8. "Then, after school [name of student] finds out that someone has been telling lies about him/her." (Still more air.)

9. Ask the student, "What do you think is about to happen to you?" (They will answer, "I'll pop/explode.") Then, using the pin, pop the balloon and discuss how this happens if you let anger/stress/frustration build up inside of you.

10. Next, explain that it is necessary to deflate and deal with little things that bother you as they happen, instead of letting them build up.

11. Pull out another balloon, and tell the same story about the same child with some additions. This time, the student in the story takes care of his/her feelings as they happen. Deflate the balloon as the student offers calming techniques. Allow students in the class or group to come up with alternatives for the incidents that make the child angry. Ask each of these students to stand and become the student's conscience in the story. Each time you tell another incident that adds to the student's anger, say, "But [name of student] heard his/her conscience say, "Take a shower" (insert the student's idea). Ask students to standby until it is their turn to become the conscience. After the students state how their conscience would choose to deflate their anger, they are asked to sit down. Some examples of alternatives to becoming angry are stated below:
    - Alarm clock goes off (inflate)—get up (deflate).
    - Late for school (inflate)—catch the bus and take a deep breath (deflate).
    - Older students teasing you (inflate)—say something funny back to them (deflate).
    - Forgotten homework (inflate)—accept the consequence and plan not to let it happen again (deflate).
    - Milk spilled on lunch (inflate)—ask for a new lunch from cafeteria workers (deflate).

- Someone is telling lies (inflate)—ask some of your friends to tell others the stories are not true (deflate).
- Books knocked down (inflate)—pick them up and say "Oh well, stuff happens like that sometime" (deflate).

VARIATIONS

1. Let each student use a balloon to demonstrate throughout the story.
2. Have students role-play or discuss other situations and brainstorm ways to deflate their anger.

FOLLOW-UP

Focus discussion on the importance of thinking of different choices available when becoming angry. Explain that we all make choices when dealing with our anger, some are appropriate, some are inappropriate. Each choice we make carries a particular consequence - some get us into more trouble, some get us in less trouble. Ask students to think about choices they can make to get themselves into less trouble. You may also ask how the students have dealt appropriately with their angry feelings in the past.

THE MEAN OLD TROLL

Grade Levels: 2-5

Time: 30 Minutes

PURPOSE

To practice brainstorming, problem solving,
and positive comebacks.

MATERIALS NEEDED

Three Billy Goats Gruff adapted review
Construction paper stepping stones
Mean Old Troll Problem Situation Cards*
Timer
Point Cards in little envelopes

*(reproduced & cutout)

OBJECT

To collect as many points as possible
when crossing the stepping stones.

PROCEDURES

1. Cutout point cards - (25, 50, 75,150, 200, etc.). Approximately eight point cards are needed per pocket. If one pocket runs out, you may return points to a pocket once they have been taken out and recorded.

2. Create construction paper stepping stones and write strategies on them (see page 50).

3. Review the story of Three Billy Goats Gruff emphasizing that the goats each used a comeback to save themselves from the mean old troll so they could cross the bridge. Discuss different examples of comebacks that can be used with others who use put-downs.

4. Divide the students into two teams.

5. Give the first student a problem situation and ask them to stand ready to move across the stones. Ask the student to read the problem situation to their team, and ask them if they have any questions about the situation. Begin the timer and allow about one minute for play.

6. Ask the standing student to move randomly to different stones, at each stone calling on one of their team members to respond to the same situation card in the manner directed by the stone. If their team does respond appropriately, the moving student may reach down and pick a point card from the pocket in the stone. The student then moves to another stone and again calls on the team for a response. Play continues as time allows. The object is to move to as many stones as possible, collecting as many points as possible before the timer runs out.

7. Teams take turns crossing on the stones.

8. Points are added at the end of the round.

VARIATION

Use three chairs as three bridges for students to cross. The team must choose a comeback at each chair to move their team member over the river.

FOLLOW-UP

Ask the students the following questions:
1. What comebacks did you feel most comfortable and successful using?
2. Could this work for you in real life? How?

The Adapted Review of
Three Billy Goats Gruff

Once upon a time, as you remember, there were Three Billy Goats Gruff who wanted to cross the bridge to eat the greener grass on the other side of a river. But a mean old troll lived under the bridge, and he threatened everyone who wanted to use his bridge. Instead of being intimidated, the smallest billy goat went first over the bridge. When the troll threatened to eat him, he made a deal with the troll, telling him if he waited for the bigger billy goat there would be more of him to eat, so it would be in the troll's best interest to let the smallest billy goat cross the bridge.

The troll agreed to the deal that the smallest billy goat made. The middle-sized billy goat made the same deal as the smallest billy goat, saying that his much bigger brother goat would soon be trying to cross the bridge.

The biggest billy goat was very assertive with the troll, he challenged the troll to try to stop him, and he stood up for himself. He was successful knocking the troll off the bridge, and crossing the bridge following his two brothers.

The billy goats learned a very important lesson in dealing with the mean old troll. They learned that you must be smart, make deals and become assertive when dealing with difficult people.

MEAN OLD TROLL

Comeback strategies with examples, for you to explain and write on stepping stones:

1. Make a deal. ("If you stop doing that, I'll play with you. If you don't stop, I won't play with you.")

2. Use humor. (Make a joke out of the put-down.)

3. Agree. ("That's O.K. I like this hair-do anyway even if you don't.")

4. Compliment. ("I like your shirt. Where did you get it?")

5. Apologize. ("I'm sorry if I've done something to offend you.")

6. Use friendly talk. ("Would you like to go play?")

7. Be assertive. ("STOP HITTING ME RIGHT NOW!")

8. Ask a distracting question. ("What time do you have?")

9. Use old sayings. ("Sticks and stones may break my bones, but words will never hurt me.")

10. Use shocked/surprised looks.

MEAN OLD TROLL POINT CARDS

Mean Old Troll Point Cards

25

Mean Old Troll Point Cards

50

Mean Old Troll Point Cards

75

Mean Old Troll Point Cards

100

Mean Old Troll Point Cards

150

Mean Old Troll Point Cards

200

Mean Old Troll Point Cards

25

Mean Old Troll Point Cards

50

MEAN OLD TROLL PROBLEM SITUATION CARDS

Mean Old Troll Situation Cards Another student calls you a name.	**Mean Old Troll Situation Cards** Someone makes fun of your nose, ears, size, etc.
Mean Old Troll Situation Cards Another student calls your mom/dad a name.	**Mean Old Troll Situation Cards** A student laughs at the grade you got on a paper.
Mean Old Troll Situation Cards Another student keeps calling you a bad name.	**Mean Old Troll Situation Cards** A friend tells you they aren't your friend anymore and says they won't play with you.
Mean Old Troll Situation Cards Someone makes fun of your hair.	**Mean Old Troll Situation Cards** Someone pushes you in line.

© 1997 by YouthLight, Inc.

Mean Old Troll Situation Cards

A friend tells all of
your friends not to
play with you.

Mean Old Troll Situation Cards

Someone knocks all of
your books out of your
hands and runs away.

Mean Old Troll Situation Cards

Another student gossips
about you to all of your
friends, and it is not true.

Mean Old Troll Situation Cards

Another student
brags about how well
they have played a game.

Mean Old Troll Situation Cards

Someone is picking
on your little
brother or sister.

Mean Old Troll Situation Cards

A student says they
don't want you on
their team because you
can't play very well.

Mean Old Troll Situation Cards

A student got in
front of you in
the lunch line.

Mean Old Troll Situation Cards

Someone brags that
they made the
Honor Roll and
you didn't.

ROCKY

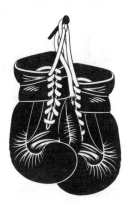

Grade Levels: 2-5

Time: 30 Minutes

PURPOSE

To teach students how to respond to teasing statements.

MATERIALS NEEDED

Dress up clothes for bad guy
Bell

OBJECT

For one student to make a comeback in the boxing ring before the count of three and earn as many points as possible.

PROCEDURES

1. Instruct the students to sit in a circle. This circle will become the "boxing ring."

2. Ask students if they remember the movies about a famous boxing star named Rocky. Briefly, students are told that Rocky was sometimes the underdog but he tried really hard and won many fights. In this game, students will not be physically fighting like Rocky, but verbally fighting with positive comebacks. Tell them the secret is to have determination and be quick to respond to keep themselves winners.

3. Choose one student to be the bad guy and dress them in clothing to represent such. One option is a motorcycle cap or helmet, glasses, chains, etc. If these articles are not available, another option is a sign hung around the student's neck.

4. Choose one student to be the good guy. This student does not put on any dress-up items.

5. Send each student to a different corner of the boxing ring. In the beginning, you play the part of the referee. Later as students learn the game, they can play referee. Begin by making a big announcement introducing the bad guy in corner number one. The class is instructed to boo this announcement. The referee then introduces the good guy in corner number two. The class is instructed to cheer this introduction. Next, the referee asks the boxers to come to center ring, shake hands, and "come out fighting" when the bell rings.

6. At center ring, the bad guy makes a put-down statement to the good guy. The good guy immediately goes "down" (squats down) for a count of three from the referee. By the time the referee gets to three, the good guy must jump up and say a comeback. Explain the rules for comebacks before the game begins. The rules are:

- No put-downs are allowed.

- Use "I" statements.

  Put-down: "Your shirt looks ugly." Comeback: "I like my shirt."

- Use humor.

  Put-down: "Your shirt looks ugly." Comeback: "Hey, I think I might have seen your shirt when I was shopping for this one. We must have the same taste in stores."

7. If the good guy offers a comeback by the count of three, the good guy gets a point. If the good guy is not able to offer a comeback by the count of three, the bad guy gets the point. (Note: The class is not broken into teams, the good guy/bad guy score is kept on the board. The object is for the good guys to win even if some matches have to be replayed for success.)

FOLLOW-UP

Focus discussion on discovering ways to come back after hearing teasing comments from friends. Teach students to be assertive when dealing with put-downs and reinforce them in the classroom for doing so.

Stone Face

Grade Levels: K-5

Time: 30 Minutes

Purpose

To practice blocking out the influence of others in order to concentrate.

Materials Needed

Small stones made out of paper

Object

To make it through a gauntlet of noisy students while maintaining a straight face.

Procedures

1. Make two lines of students facing each other to form a gauntlet. Explain the Native American's practice in some tribes of running the gauntlet in order to save one's life. Native Americans would allow some prisoners who showed courage to run the gauntlet. Two lines of Native Americans facing each other had weapons to use on the prisoner running the gauntlet. If the prisoner made it alive to the end of the run between the two lines, his/her life was spared.

2. Choose one student to walk between the two lines. While the student is walking, the ones in each line try to distract the student to make that student look at them or smile. No touching of the student in the middle is allowed. Distractions can include funny faces, friendly cat calls or noises. All distractions must be appropriate.

3. If the student makes it to the end of the gauntlet without being distracted, he/she wins a small stone to keep as a reminder to keep a stone face in the classroom while concentrating on classroom tasks.

4. Drawing a face on their paper stones can also be done as an extra reminder of the stone face they preserved.

FOLLOW-UP

Ask the students the following questions:

- What made it difficult or easy to keep a stone face in the gauntlet?

- What helped you concentrate while in the gauntlet?

- How can you use this skill in the classroom?

- How can you use this skill with other students who tease you or pick on you?

FOOTBALL

Grade Levels: 2-5

Time: 30 Minutes

PURPOSE

To teach students to deal with teasing using humor, being assertive, being agreeable, and complimenting the aggressor.

MATERIALS NEEDED

Football marker
Soft squeeze football
Football field drawn on blackboard or poster
Timer
Marker envelopes
Football Situation Cards (Reproduced & cutout)

OBJECT

To respond correctly to
Football Situation Cards
and make touchdowns.

PROCEDURES

1. Draw a large football field on the blackboard or poster board with clearly placed ten yard markers (see page 60).

2. Draw two people or use paper clips or tape to attach teams to the football field to represent the teams as they move down the field.

3. Reproduce situation marker cards. (The card categories listed below are described in procedure four.) The purpose of the card is to advance the teams up or down the field.
   a. 10 yard marker cards deal with agreement responses.
   b. 20 yard marker cards deal with complimentary or change the subject responses.

c. 30 yard marker cards deal with assertive responses.

d. 40 yard marker cards deal with humorous responses.

e. Field goal situation cards deal with other responses.

4. Divide the class into two teams. Place marker cards in the little boxes or marker envelopes close to the football field, each stating their yardage value. Choose one team to begin the game. The situation marker cards are described below. Each description should serve as a guideline of how children must respond to each question.

a. Agreement response - The student responds, "You're right." For example, if the aggressor teases, "You have big feet," the agreement response would be, "You're right, they are pretty big. I'll let you know if they get any bigger." This response is effective because it not only catches the teaser off guard, but also gives the teaser absolutely nothing to argue with the other student about.

b. Complimentary or change the subject response - The student responds by changing the subject to a mutual topic of interest causing the teaser to think of something else. For example, if the teaser pushes a student in line, the complimentary or change the subject response would be, "Man, you're pretty strong, you must be a great football player. Do you like to play?"

c. Assertive response - The student responds by making the teaser aware of how they are making him/her feel, asking him/her to stop in a friendly way, asking him/her in a firm way, stating his/her intentions of not fighting, reminding the teaser of school consequences should a fight occur, or any other response that would indicate a firm stand. For example, if a teaser continues to nudge a student in line, the assertive response would be, "Hey man, knock it off. You know we'll both miss recess if we keep it up."

d. Humor - The students could use humor to help lighten an otherwise tense situation. For example, if the teaser says, "It looks like you get your clothes at a cheap store." the humorous response would be, "Well, we obviously have the same taste in clothes. I thought I saw your outfit there when I was shopping. Maybe we can go shopping together sometime." Another humorous response would be to tell a joke or funny story to get the teaser's mind off teasing. This incorporates changing the subject along with using humor to get the teaser to quit.

e. Other responses - The student uses responses ranging from ignoring, to walking away, to playing with someone else, to getting an adult to help, to talking to someone about their feelings. Any other response which does not include fighting is also acceptable.

5. Choose a team to go first. Ask one player to come to the front of the room. When you say, "go" and begin the timer (set for one minute or so), this player will throw the football to a player on their team. The player who catches it runs to the front of the room and chooses a card from any one of the envelopes. This player can respond to the card by him/herself or ask a teammate to help. The team starts from the 0 yard marker which is furthest from their goal and moves the amount of yards stated on their card. For example, if the team starts on the 0 yard marker (see A in the diagram below), and answers a 40 yard situation card, this would take their team to the 40 yard marker (see diagram B below). If the player then answers a 30 yard situation card, the team advances to the 30 yard marker (see C in the diagram below). Play continues until time runs out or a touchdown occurs. If time runs out before a touchdown, the other team picks up the ball where the other team left it and goes the other way. For example, if the ball is at C on the diagram on the 30 yard marker and time runs out, the other team would get the ball there and go the other way towards A on the diagram. If the team makes a touchdown, they are awarded six points. They have the option to choose a question from the packet of cards designated as other response. If they take this option, the team has a chance to receive the extra point if they answer correctly.

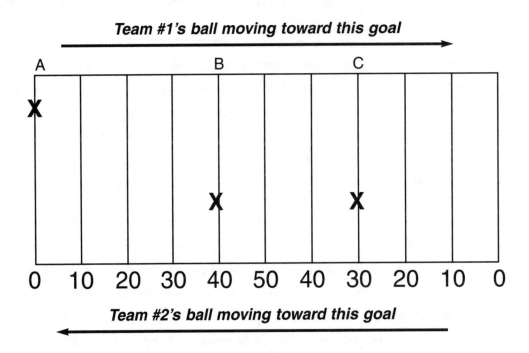

6. Any team using threats, angry responses, put-downs, fights, or other violent answers is penalized -10 yards.

7. Play continues until you call time.

FOLLOW-UP

Ask students to consider which responses were more difficult, which were more practical, which they currently use, which they could not use, which they need to develop. You may ask the students to do a final review of the types of responses taught during the game. Ask the students to try one of these responses the next time a teaser approaches them.

10 YARD MARKER FOOTBALL SITUATION CARDS (AGREEMENT)

10 Yard Marker Football Agreement Cards

SOMEONE SAYS YOUR FEET ARE BIG.

10 Yard Marker Football Agreement Cards

SOMEONE SAYS YOUR SHOES ARE NERDY.

10 Yard Marker Football Agreement Cards

SOMEONE SAYS YOUR HAIRCUT IS UGLY.

10 Yard Marker Football Agreement Cards

SOMEONE SAYS YOU HAVE A BOYFRIEND OR GIRLFRIEND.

10 Yard Marker Football Agreement Cards

SOMEONE SAYS YOU HAVE BIG EARS.

10 Yard Marker Football Agreement Cards

SOMEONE SAYS YOU'RE TOO TALL

10 Yard Marker Football Agreement Cards

SOMEONE SAYS YOU CAN'T SING.

10 Yard Marker Football Agreement Cards

SOMEONE SAYS YOU EAT WORMS

10 Yard Marker Football Agreement Cards

SOMEONE SAYS YOUR PAPER LOOKS CRUMPLED

10 Yard Marker Football Agreement Cards

SOMEONE SAYS YOU LIKE A GIRL OR BOY AND YOU REALLY DON'T.

10 Yard Marker Football Agreement Cards

SOMEONE SAYS YOU THINK YOU'RE SMART.

10 Yard Marker Football Agreement Cards

SOMEONE SAYS YOUR HAIR MAKE YOUR CHEEKS LOOK BIG.

10 Yard Marker Football Agreement Cards

SOMEONE SAYS YOUR CLOTHES ARE TOO BIG.

10 Yard Marker Football Agreement Cards

SOMEONE SAYS YOU GET YOUR CLOTHES AT A CHEAP STORE.

POWER PLAY

10 Yard Marker Football Agreement Cards

10 Yard Marker Football Agreement Cards

SOMEONE SAYS YOUR SHOES ARE STUPID.

SOMEONE SAYS YOU'RE TOO SHORT.

20 YARD MARKER FOOTBALL SITUATION CARDS
(COMPLIMENT OR CHANGE THE SUBJECT)

20 Yard Marker Football Compliment Cards

20 Yard Marker Football Compliment Cards

SOMEONE PUSHES YOU IN LINE.

SOMEONE SAYS YOUR SHOES ARE NERDY.

20 Yard Marker Football Compliment Cards

20 Yard Marker Football Compliment Cards

SOMEONE SAYS YOUR HAIRCUT IS TOO NAPPY.

SOMEONE KEEPS LOOKING AT YOU IN A FUNNY WAY.

20 Yard Marker Football Compliment Cards

SOMEONE PULLS YOUR HAIR.

20 Yard Marker Football Compliment Cards

SOMEONE SAYS YOU'RE STUPID.

20 Yard Marker Football Compliment Cards

SOMEONE KEEPS ASKING YOU TO PLAY BALL.

20 Yard Marker Football Compliment Cards

SOMEONE SAYS YOU ARE A NERD.

20 Yard Marker Football Compliment Cards

SOMEONE GRABS AT YOUR PAPER.

20 Yard Marker Football Compliment Cards

SOMEONE SAYS YOU LIKE A GIRL OR BOY YOU REALLY DON'T.

20 Yard Marker Football Compliment Cards

SOMEONE IS ALWAYS TRYING TO BREAK IN FRONT OF YOU IN LINE.

20 Yard Marker Football Compliment Cards

SOMEONE SAYS YOUR HAIR LOOKS BAD.

© 1997 by YouthLight, Inc.

20 Yard Marker Football Compliment Cards

20 Yard Marker Football Compliment Cards

SOMEONE CALLS YOUR CLOTHES ARE STUPID.

SOMEONE SAYS YOUR CLOTHES ARE CHEAP.

20 Yard Marker Football Compliment Cards

20 Yard Marker Football Compliment Cards

SOMEONE IS TOUCHING YOUR FOOT.

SOMEONE HAS THEIR HAND ON YOUR DESK.

30 YARD MARKER FOOTBALL SITUATION CARDS
(ASSERTIVE)

30 Yard Marker Football Assertive Cards

30 Yard Marker Football Assertive Cards

SOMEONE BREAKS IN FRONT OF YOU PLAYING JUMP ROPE.

SOMEONE THREATENS TO BEAT YOU UP.

30 Yard Marker Football Assertive Cards

SOMEONE TRIES TO COPY YOUR PAPER.

30 Yard Marker Football Assertive Cards

SOMEONE TAKES YOUR LUNCH MONEY.

30 Yard Marker Football Assertive Cards

SOMEONE PUSHES YOU IN LINE.

30 Yard Marker Football Assertive Cards

SOMEONE THREATENS TO HURT YOU IN THE BATHROOM.

30 Yard Marker Football Assertive Cards

SOMEONE TALKS BADLY ABOUT YOUR MOM.

30 Yard Marker Football Assertive Cards

SOMEONE TAKES YOUR WALLET OR PURSE.

30 Yard Marker Football Assertive Cards

SOMEONE TALKS BADLY ABOUT YOU.

30 Yard Marker Football Assertive Cards

SOMEONE THREATENS TO TELL ON YOU IF YOU DON'T GIVE THEM YOUR LUNCH MONEY.

POWER PLAY

68

30 Yard Marker Football Assertive Cards

SOMEONE TALKS BADLY ABOUT YOUR GRANDMA.

30 Yard Marker Football Assertive Cards

SOMEONE WON'T PLAY WITH YOU ANYMORE.

30 Yard Marker Football Assertive Cards

SOMEONE SAYS YOU ARE STUPID.

30 Yard Marker Football Assertive Cards

SOMEONE THREATENS TO HURT YOU IF YOU DON'T GIVE THEM YOUR SNACK.

30 Yard Marker Football Assertive Cards

SOMEONE TAKES YOUR PENCIL.

30 Yard Marker Football Assertive Cards

SOMEONE PINCHES YOU.

30 Yard Marker Football Assertive Cards

SOMEONE ASKS YOU TO GIVE THEM THE ANSWERS ON A TEST.

30 Yard Marker Football Assertive Cards

SOMEONE TELLS YOU NOT TO TELL THAT THEY DID SOMETHING AGAINST THE RULES.

POWER PLAY

40 Yard Marker Football Situation Cards (Humor)

40 Yard Marker Football Humor Cards

SOMEONE CALLS YOU A NERD.

40 Yard Marker Football Humor Cards

SOMEONE SAYS YOUR MOM IS TOO FAT.

40 Yard Marker Football Humor Cards

SOMEONE SAYS YOU STINK.

40 Yard Marker Football Humor Cards

SOMEONE SAYS YOU LIKE SNOT.

40 Yard Marker Football Humor Cards

SOMEONE SAYS YOUR HAIR IS OUT OF STYLE.

40 Yard Marker Football Humor Cards

SOMEONE SAYS YOUR MOM IS TOO SKINNY.

70

40 Yard Marker Football Humor Cards

SOMEONE SAYS YOU ARE A JERK.

40 Yard Marker Football Humor Cards

SOMEONE SAYS YOU EAT WORMS.

40 Yard Marker Football Humor Cards

SOMEONE SAYS YOUR CLOTHES ARE DIRTY.

40 Yard Marker Football Humor Cards

SOMEONE SAYS YOUR DAD IS A LOSER.

40 Yard Marker Football Humor Cards

SOMEONE SAYS THEY DON'T LIKE YOU.

40 Yard Marker Football Humor Cards

SOMEONE SAYS YOU LIVE IN AN UGLY HOUSE.

40 Yard Marker Football Humor Cards

SOMEONE SAYS YOU WON'T PASS YOUR GRADE.

40 Yard Marker Football Humor Cards

SOMEONE SAYS YOUR FEET ARE TOO BIG.

40 Yard Marker Football Humor Cards

SOMEONE SAYS YOU HAVE COOTIES.

40 Yard Marker Football Humor Cards

SOMEONE SAYS YOU LIKE BUGARS.

FIELD GOAL FOOTBALL SITUATION CARDS (OTHER RESPONSES)

Field Goal Football Other Responses Cards

SOMEONE KEEPS STEALING THE BALL.

Field Goal Football Other Responses Cards

SOMEONE CALLS YOU A NAME.

Field Goal Football Other Responses Cards

SOMEONE WON'T PLAY WITH YOU.

Field Goal Football Other Responses Cards

SOMEONE ROLLS THEIR EYES AT YOU.

Field Goal Football Other Responses Cards

SOMEONE KEEPS KICKING YOUR FOOT.

Field Goal Football Other Responses Cards

SOMEONE BREAKS IN FRONT OF YOU GOING TO THE GYM.

Field Goal Football Other Responses Cards

SOMEONE DOESN'T INVITE YOU TO A PARTY.

Field Goal Football Other Responses Cards

SOMEONE LOOKS NEGATIVELY AT YOU.

Field Goal Football Other Responses Cards

SOMEONE TALKS TO YOU ALL THE TIME.

Field Goal Football Other Responses Cards

SOMEONE SAYS YOU ARE AN IDIOT.

Field Goal Football Other Responses Cards

SOMEONE SAYS YOU HAVE LICE.

Field Goal Football Other Responses Cards

SOMEONE KEEPS TAPPING YOU ON THE SHOULDER.

Field Goal Football Other Responses Cards

SOMEONE TRIES TO COPY YOUR PAPER.

Field Goal Football Other Responses Cards

SOMEONE SAYS YOU ARE A WIMP

Field Goal Football Other Responses Cards

SOMEONE SAYS YOU ARE DUMB.

Field Goal Football Other Responses Cards

SOMEONE INTERRUPTS YOU WHEN YOU'RE TALKING.

Field Goal Football Other Responses Cards

SOMEONE SAYS NO ONE WILL PLAY WITH YOU.

Field Goal Football Other Responses Cards

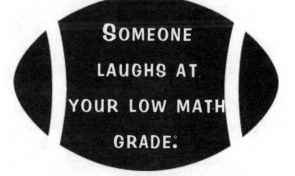

SOMEONE LAUGHS AT YOUR LOW MATH GRADE.

Field Goal Football Other Responses Cards

SOMEONE SAYS THEY WON'T BE YOUR FRIEND ANYMORE

Field Goal Football Other Responses Cards

SOMEONE LOOKS AT YOU FUNNY.

Section II:

Making decisions is an integral part of every student's life. The decision-making process is determined by the thinking and reasoning abilities of the student as well as their ability to view the outcomes and consequences of past decisions. Encouraging students to evaluate their decisions and the effects their decisions have upon their life is crucial if growth is to occur. Teaching problem-solving methods is essential to assure that students understand this process of making decisions and evaluating the consequences.

The games and activities that follow will help students understand this problem-solving process. They will allow students to practice responses and enable them to make quick decisions when faced with tough life choices. Some activities call for students to make fast decisions; some activities teach the problem-solving process; and one activity focuses on practicing decisions students might be asked to make later in life. All activities ask the students to evaluate their own decision-making process while encouraging them to make positive decisions about their own lives.

DECISION MAKING

RED FLAG

Grade Levels: K-5   **Time: 30 Minutes**

PURPOSES

To help students recognize situations that could get them into trouble or endanger them. To help students walk away from dangerous situations.

MATERIALS NEEDED

Red Flag Positive & Negative Situation Cards
(reproduced & cutout)
Red Flag
(made with construction paper & popsicle stick)
Stool or Chair

OBJECT

To grab the flag before your opponent, walk away and correctly identify what is dangerous about the situation described.

PROCEDURES

1. Mix Red Flag Positive and Negative Situation Cards and place them in a stack.

2. Divide students into two teams.

3. Ask each team to send a teammate to face a member from the other team with their hands behind their backs and a red flag on a stool, chair, or student desk between them.

4. Read a situation card out loud.

5. The team member who first recognizes the dangerous situation, grabs the red flag, turns and walks to a designated area and then explains what was dangerous about the situation wins one point for their team.

6. A point is lost if they grab the flag after a positive situation card is read, and they can't identify the danger in the situation.

VARIATION

Place the red flag on a small table with two chairs placed side by side about 10 - 15 feet from the table. When the situation card is read, the two team members race to the table to grab the flag.

FOLLOW-UP

Ask the students the following questions:

- How did it feel to walk away from danger?

- What would make it difficult for you to walk away in a real situation?

- From which situation or sign of danger would it be the most difficult for you to walk away?

- How did you feel when you got the flag and walked away before the student facing you?

RED FLAG NEGATIVE SITUATION CARDS

Red Flag Negative Situation Cards

TWO PEOPLE ARE ARGUING ABOUT WHAT TO PLAY OR HOW TO PLAY.

Red Flag Negative Situation Cards

SOMEONE SAYS, "YOUR DAD IS NO GOOD."

Red Flag Negative Situation Cards

ONE PERSON WANTS TO BE FIRST IN LINE ALL THE TIME.

Red Flag Negative Situation Cards

SOMEONE SAYS, "YOU DON'T KNOW ANYTHING."

Red Flag Negative Situation Cards

ONE PERSON PUSHES ANOTHER PERSON.

Red Flag Negative Situation Cards

SOMEONE SAYS, "NOBODY LIKES YOU."

Red Flag Negative Situation Cards

SOMEONE SAYS, "YOU THINK YOU'RE TOUGH, DON'T YOU?"

Red Flag Negative Situation Cards

SOMEONE SAYS, "GO HOME. WE DON'T WANT TO PLAY WITH YOU"

78

Red Flag Negative Situation Cards	Red Flag Negative Situation Cards
SOMEONE ASKS, "WANT TO FIGHT?"	**SOMEONE SAYS, "GET OUT OF MY WAY."**
Red Flag Negative Situation Cards	Red Flag Negative Situation Cards
SOMEONE SAYS, "YOUR MOM IS UGLY."	**SOMEONE SAYS, "YOU'RE STUPID."**
Red Flag Negative Situation Cards	Red Flag Negative Situation Cards
SOMEONE ROLLS THEIR EYES AT YOU.	**SOMEONE LAUGHS AT YOUR CREATIVE WRITING STORY.**
Red Flag Negative Situation Cards	Red Flag Negative Situation Cards
SOMEONE SAYS, "I'M GOING TO HIT YOUR LITTLE BROTHER."	**SOMEONE SAYS, "YOU HAVE COOTIES."**

Red Flag Positive Situation Cards

Red Flag Positive Situation Cards

**SOMEONE SAYS,
"YOU'RE MY FRIEND."**

Red Flag Positive Situation Cards

**SOMEONE SAYS,
"IT'S YOUR TURN."**

Red Flag Positive Situation Cards

**SOMEONE SAYS,
"I'LL HELP YOU DO YOUR
MATH ASSIGNMENT."**

Red Flag Positive Situation Cards

**SOMEONE ASKS,
"DO YOU WANT TO
PLAY BALL?"**

Red Flag Positive Situation Cards

**SOMEONE SAYS,
"I'LL SHARE MY
POPCORN WITH YOU."**

Red Flag Positive Situation Cards

**SOMEONE SAYS,
"WHAT A GREAT TIME
I'VE HAD WITH YOU."**

Red Flag Positive Situation Cards

**SOMEONE SAYS,
"YOU'RE MY BUDDY."**

Red Flag Positive Situation Cards

**SOMEONE SAYS,
"THANKS FOR HELPING ME
WITH MY MATH."**

Red Flag Positive Situation Cards

SOMEONE ASKS,
"WHAT TIME IS IT?"

Red Flag Positive Situation Cards

SOMEONE SAYS,
"I LIKE HOW YOU LET
ME IN FRONT OF YOU
IN LINE."

Red Flag Positive Situation Cards

SOMEONE SAYS,
"I'M SORRY I BUMPED INTO
YOU."

Red Flag Positive Situation Cards

SOMEONE ASKS,
"MAY I BORROW
A PENCIL."

Red Flag Positive Situation Cards

SOMEONE ASKS,
"THANK YOU FOR
GIVING ME THE SALT."

Red Flag Positive Situation Cards

SOMEONE SAYS,
"PLEASE PASS THE GLUE."

Red Flag Positive Situation Cards

SOMEONE SAYS,
"EXCUSE ME FOR
STEPPING ON YOUR FOOT."

Red Flag Positive Situation Cards

SOMEONE ASKS,
"CONGRATULATIONS FOR
MAKING THE HONOR ROLL."

THE THREE BEARS

Grade Levels: K-2

Time: 30 Minutes

PURPOSE
To help students recognize good and bad decisions.

MATERIALS NEEDED
One set of three bowls or pictures of bowls
Response Cards (reproduced & cutout)
Adapted Review of The Three Bears

OBJECT
To determine, by vote, which response cards are hot, cold, or just right decisions.

PROCEDURES

1. Divide the group into two teams and review the story of the Three Bears.

2. The teams take turns taking cards with situation prompts on them. Cards depict three types of decisions - hot (it will get you into trouble), cold (it makes no sense), and just right (it is good and will keep you out of trouble). The correct answer is marked.

3. Ask one team member to read the response card to the other team, or read it for them yourself. The responding team must say what kind of decision it is by voting with a show of hands. For example, after reading the response, the student may hold the card over each bowl for a vote.

4. If the majority of students vote correctly, the card is then placed into the corresponding bowl. Give the team one point for each correct answer. If the majority of students on the team vote incorrectly, the card is put back at the bottom of the stack. No points are earned.

5.   The winning team has the most points.

VARIATION

Let individuals on the team answer the response cards instead of determining an answer as a group.

FOLLOW-UP

Ask the students the following questions:

- Which decision was the most difficult for you?

- Which decision was the easiest for you?

- Why are good decisions important?

- How would you feel if you were the only one making a just right decision?

- What helped you to decide on the just right decisions?

The Adapted Review of
The Three Bears

Once upon a time, as you remember, there was a little girl named Goldilocks who wandered into The Three Bears' house in the woods while the Bears were out taking a walk. Goldilocks made several decisions while she was in the house. First, she decided which porridge to eat. Papa Bear's porridge was too hot, Goldilocks could have burned herself if she ate it, which would have been painful. Mama Bear's porridge was too cold, and it would have tasted awful. However, Baby Bear's porridge was just right, so she ate it after deciding the consequences of the other two choices.

As you remember, there were other choices Goldilocks made such as which chair to sit on, and which bed to sleep on. Goldilocks made each decision carefully, weighing all the consequences.

In the end, Goldilocks was scared away when the Three Bears returned home. Do you think she made the right decision to enter the Three Bears' house without their permission in the first place?

Decisions are sometimes made because they feel right at the time. It is important, however, to think about the long-range consequences and how they might affect other people as well as ourselves before making important decisions.

RESPONSE CARDS FOR THE THREE BEARS

 Response Cards for The Three Bears

RUNNING IN THE HALL
HOT

 Response Cards for The Three Bears

TRYING TO SMOKE
HOT

 Response Cards for The Three Bears

TURNING IN HOMEWORK
JUST RIGHT

 Response Cards for The Three Bears

SAYING, "PLEASE"
JUST RIGHT

Response Cards for The Three Bears

SAYING, "THANK YOU"
JUST RIGHT

 Response Cards for The Three Bears

CHASING THE CAT
HOT OR COLD

Response Cards for The Three Bears

YELLING AT FRIENDS
HOT

 Response Cards for The Three Bears

TEARING UP
SCHOOL PROPERTY
HOT

 Response Cards for The Three Bears

KICKING THE DOG
HOT OR COLD

 Response Cards for The Three Bears

TEARING UP A
SHEET OF PAPER THAT HAS
A SMALL MISTAKE ON IT
COLD

 Response Cards for The Three Bears

EATING TOO MUCH FOOD
COLD

 Response Cards for The Three Bears

MAKING FUN OF A FRIEND
HOT

 Response Cards for The Three Bears

ACTING LIKE A BABY
COLD

 Response Cards for The Three Bears

WANTING YOUR
WAY ALL TIME
HOT OR COLD

86

Response Cards for The Three Bears

YELLING AT A

SISTER OR BROTHER

HOT OR **COLD**

Response Cards for The Three Bears

TELLING ON

SOMEONE WITHOUT

FIRST TRYING TO

HANDLE IT YOURSELF

COLD

Response Cards for The Three Bears

NOT TEASING

SOMEONE WHO IS

DIFFERENT

JUST RIGHT

Response Cards for The Three Bears

PUSHING IN LINE

HOT

Response Cards for The Three Bears

BRINGING THE

MATERIALS THAT YOU

NEED TO CLASS

JUST RIGHT

Response Cards for The Three Bears

NOT DOING YOUR

CLASSWORK

COLD

Response Cards for The Three Bears

SHARING A PENCIL

WITH SOMEONE

WHO NEEDS ONE

JUST RIGHT

Response Cards for The Three Bears

GIVING UGLY

SIGNS WITH YOUR HANDS

HOT

Response Cards for The Three Bears

HELPING SOMEONE UNDERSTAND THE DIRECTIONS ON AN ASSIGNMENT
JUST RIGHT

Response Cards for The Three Bears

BRAGGING ABOUT WINNING A GAME
HOT

Response Cards for The Three Bears

MINDING YOUR OWN BUSINESS AND TAKING CARE OF YOURSELF
JUST RIGHT

Response Cards for The Three Bears

TAKING SOMEONE'S PENCIL WITHOUT ASKING
HOT

Response Cards for The Three Bears

BRINGING THE MATERIALS THAT YOU NEED TO CLASS
JUST RIGHT

Response Cards for The Three Bears

TALKING WHEN THE TEACHER HAS ASKED YOU TO BE QUIET
COLD

Response Cards for The Three Bears

SHARING PAPER WITH SOMEONE WHO NEEDS SOME
JUST RIGHT

Response Cards for The Three Bears

CUSSING
HOT

TAKE A STAND

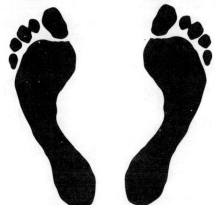

Grade Levels: 2-5

Time: 30 Minutes

PURPOSE
To practice making a decision.

MATERIALS NEEDED
Opinion Statement Cards (reproduced & cutout)

OBJECT
To sit beside, sit on, or stand on chairs as a response to an opinion statement.

PROCEDURES

1. Read Opinion Statement Cards aloud to the class or group.

2. Instruct students that if they agree with the opinion statement, they should stand up on their chairs. If they disagree with the opinion statement, they should sit on the floor next to their chairs. If they are unsure, they should remain seated in their chairs.

3. One at a time, ask several students to share their reasons for taking the stand they did on the opinion statements.

4. If any students want to change their minds after discussion has taken place, let them share what helped them change with the class.

VARIATION

The students could go to different sides of the room to denote opinions. For example, they could go to the right side if they agree, to the left side if they disagree, and to the middle if they aren't sure.

FOLLOW-UP

Ask the students the following questions:

- Which decision was the most difficult for you to make?

- Which decision was the easiest for you to make?

- Did it make a difference to you if your friends chose another decision which was different from yours?

- Did it make a difference to you if you were part of a small group who made a certain decision?

- How do your beliefs or opinions affect the way you behave?

OPINION STATEMENTS FOR TAKE A STAND

Opinion Statements for
Take a Stand

WE NEED TO ENFORCE THE RULES ON BEHAVIOR THAT WE ALREADY HAVE.

Opinion Statements for
Take a Stand

LEARNING IS IMPORTANT LATER IN LIFE.

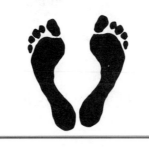

Opinion Statements for
Take a Stand

WE NEED MORE RULES AT SCHOOL ABOUT BEHAVIOR.

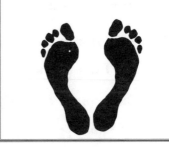

Opinion Statements for
Take a Stand

TEACHERS HELP YOU WHEN YOU NEED IT.

Opinion Statements for
Take a Stand

WE HAVE TOO MANY PARTIES AT SCHOOL.

Opinion Statements for
Take a Stand

PEOPLE WATCH TOO MUCH TV.

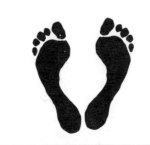

Opinion Statements for
Take a Stand

WE NEED MORE

TESTS AT SCHOOL.

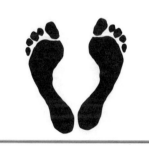

Opinion Statements for
Take a Stand

WHAT YOU LEARN IN

SCHOOL WILL HELP

YOU WHEN YOU

WANT TO GET A JOB.

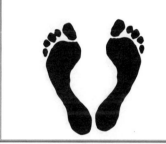

Opinion Statements for
Take a Stand

MOST CLASSES ARE

FUN TO BE IN.

Opinion Statements for
Take a Stand

HOMEWORK HELPS

YOU PRACTICE

SKILLS AND BECOME

BETTER.

Opinion Statements for
Take a Stand

BOYS ARE SMARTER

THAN GIRLS.

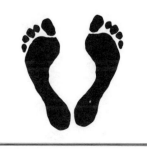

Opinion Statements for
Take a Stand

IF I BROKE A

WINDOW, I WOULD

TELL MY PARENTS.

92

Opinion Statements for
Take a Stand

GIRLS ARE SMARTER THAN BOYS.

Opinion Statements for
Take a Stand

IF I WERE AT A PARTY AND BEER WAS OFFERED TO ME, I WOULDN'T DRINK IT.

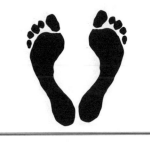

Opinion Statements for
Take a Stand

WHITE PEOPLE ARE NERDS.

Opinion Statements for
Take a Stand

IF SOMEONE MADE FUN OF MY FRIEND, I WOULD HELP MY FRIEND.

Opinion Statements for
Take a Stand

BLACK PEOPLE ARE MEAN.

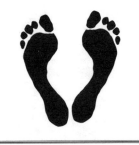

Opinion Statements for
Take a Stand

FIGHTING IS ALWAYS ALL RIGHT.

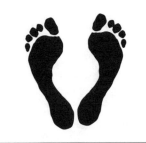

Opinion Statements for
Take a Stand

HONESTY IS GREAT.

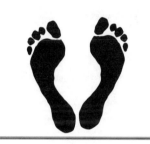

Opinion Statements for
Take a Stand

I WOULD LET MY BEST FRIEND COPY THE ANSWERS ON MY PAPER.

Opinion Statements for
Take a Stand

I WOULD TELL ON MY FRIEND IF HE WERE BREAKING THE RULES.

Opinion Statements for
Take a Stand

TEACHERS TRY TO GET YOU IN TROUBLE BY ALWAYS TRYING TO CATCH YOU BEING BAD.

Opinion Statements for
Take a Stand

IF EVERYONE TRIES SMOKING IN MY GROUP, I WOULD TRY IT JUST ONCE TOO.

Opinion Statements for
Take a Stand

IF SOMEONE KEEPS ON PICKING ON YOU, IT'S OK TO HIT HIM.

GOING FOR THE GOAL

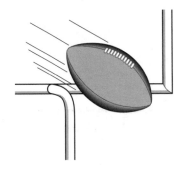

Grade Levels: 4-8   **Time: 30 Minutes**

PURPOSE
To help students set goals and solve problems.

MATERIALS NEEDED
Problem Situation Cards (reproduced & cutout)
Bell or other noise maker
Die

OBJECT
To brainstorm as a team and come up with a workable solution to a problem before the other teams.

PROCEDURES

1. Divide the students into 12 small groups. Give the numbers 1-6 to the teams with two teams each having the same number.

2. Read a problem situation from the situation cards.

3. Ask each group or team to discuss the problem for a limited time (one to three minutes). Encourage the students to brainstorm. For example, a student is not doing his/her homework. (Possible solutions are: bring home all books, call a friend for help, have a certain study space at home, have a set time for doing homework, etc.)

4. As soon as each team reaches several solutions, throw the die and call on the two teams with that number. Those two teams send a member up to ring the bell.

5. Give points to the team that rings the bell first and has a workable solution or solutions.

VARIATION

Before sending up a member of the group to ring the bell, the group must come up with three different workable solutions to the problem.

FOLLOW-UP

Ask the students the following questions:

- What helped you to solve a problem?

- How could you use the skill of problem solving in the class room? With friends? With homework?

PROBLEM SITUATIONS FOR GOING FOR THE GOAL

Problem Situation Cards for Going for the Goal

A STUDENT IS NOT DOING HIS/HER HOMEWORK.

Problem Situation Cards for Going for the Goal

THE WORK IN A CERTAIN SUBJECT IS TOO HARD.

Problem Situation Cards for Going for the Goal

A STUDENT HAS A FIGHT WITH HIS/HER BEST FRIEND.

Problem Situation Cards for Going for the Goal

A STUDENT IS YELLING OUT IN CLASS AND NOT WAITING FOR HIS/HER TURN.

Problem Situation Cards for Going for the Goal

A STUDENT DOESN'T LIKE THE TEACHER.

Problem Situation Cards for Going for the Goal

A STUDENT TALKS BACK TO THE TEACHER.

Problem Situation Cards for Going for the Goal

FRIENDS THAT USUALLY PLAY WITH A STUDENT TELL HIM/HER THAT THEY WON'T PLAY WITH THEM ANYMORE.

Problem Situation Cards for Going for the Goal

A STUDENT IS HAVING A PROBLEM AT HOME WITH HIS/HER PARENTS.

Problem Situation Cards for Going for the Goal

A FRIEND KEEPS WANTING TO COPY A STUDENT'S WORK.

Problem Situation Cards for Going for the Goal

A STUDENT IS GETTING A LOW GRADE IN A CLASS BECAUSE HE/SHE DOESN'T LIKE THE TEACHER.

Problem Situation Cards for Going for the Goal

ONE STUDENT IS A BULLY AND PICKS ON EVERYONE BY PUSHING, THREATENING, OR VERBALLY ABUSING OTHERS.

Problem Situation Cards for Going for the Goal

OTHER STUDENTS ARE TALKING ABOUT A STUDENT'S MOM SINCE SHE CAME TO SCHOOL TODAY.

SOLVING PROBLEMS BASEBALL GAME

Grade Levels: 2-5

Time: 30 Minutes

PURPOSES

- To teach problem-solving skills and brainstorming for use in social situations.

- To demonstrate there are always several ways of dealing with problems.

- To give visual demonstrations that focus on the fact that solutions actually move you closer to solving the problem.

MATERIALS NEEDED

Four sheets of paper to use as bases
Three boxes for the outfield
Soft squeeze ball
Baseball Situation Cards (reproduced & cutout)
Timer

OBJECT

To throw the ball into a situation box, and have your team provide four correct responses while you go from base to base, earning a run.

PROCEDURES

1. Divide the children into two teams.

2. Make bases and place them in the appropriate order to represent home, first, second and third base. Place three boxes in the outfield to signify the outfield positions.

3. Place one-third of the Baseball Situation Cards into each of the three boxes in the outfield.

4. The first student to bat comes up to home plate. This student has three chances to throw the ball into one of the boxes in the outfield. If the student throws the ball into one of the boxes, the student is allowed to choose a situation card from that box. If the student is unable to get the ball into one of the outfield boxes after three turns, the team loses their turn for that round. Consider the throws strikes, each team will get one out or one turn. After the out, play goes to the other team.

5. Once the student picks a card, ask them to bring the card to you. Read the situation card, and check to see if the student and team understand the question.

6. Turn over the sand timer when the team indicates they are ready to begin.

7. The team's job is to think of four alternative responses to this particular problem that might be appropriate. Ask all team members to think of correct responses, raise their hands and as they are called on by the batter, share this response with the batter. The leader must be able to hear the response in order for it to be deemed acceptable. As someone thinks of the first response, the batter is moved to first base. As someone thinks of a second appropriate response, the batter moves to second. A third correct response moves the batter to third, and the final correct response moves the batter to home. If the team is able to think of four responses before the timer runs out, the team is awarded a run. Play then goes to the other team.

8. At the end of the inning or run, ask the moving player which response he/she might choose as a response to the problem.

9. Play continues as time allows.

VARIATION

Use a sponge bat and ball and let the batter hit the ball as a pitcher from the other team pitches to the batter. If the ball is hit, the batter takes a card and answers as in the regular way of the game.

FOLLOW-UP

Ask the students the following questions:

- Do you think there are usually solutions to problems? When wouldn't there be?

- Do you ever have to try more than one solution to a problem?

- Sometimes things are out of our control, like people dying or parents divorcing. Since we can't fix these things because they are out of our control, what kind of things can we do that are in our control to help these situations?

BASEBALL SITUATION CARDS

Baseball Situation Cards

YOUR FRIEND IS ALWAYS COMPLAINING ABOUT HIS/HER NAME BEING ON THE BOARD FOR BAD BEHAVIOR. WHAT FOUR THINGS COULD YOU SUGGEST THE HE/SHE DO?

Baseball Situation Cards

YOU NOTICE SOMEONE IN YOUR CLASS DOES NOT HAVE ANY FRIENDS. THEY ASK YOU HOW TO MAKE FRIENDS. NAME FOUR WAYS TO MAKE FRIENDS.

Baseball Situation Cards

YOUR FRIEND IS SAD. WHAT FOUR THINGS COULD YOU SUGGEST THE HE/SHE DO?

Baseball Situation Cards

YOU'RE AFRAID YOU'RE GOING TO FAIL YOUR GRADE. NAME FOUR THINGS YOU COULD DO TO PREVENT THIS FROM HAPPENING.

Baseball Situation Cards

YOUR FRIEND IS ANGRY. WHAT FOUR THINGS COULD YOU SUGGEST THAT HE/SHE DO?

Baseball Situation Cards

YOU REALLY FEEL STRESSED OUT DURING A TEST. NAME FOUR WAYS TO RELAX WHEN YOU FEEL THIS WAY.

Baseball Situation Cards

NAME FOUR THINGS SOMEONE COULD DO TO HAVE FUN WITHOUT TAKING DRUGS.

Baseball Situation Cards

YOU MOM AND DAD ARE GETTING A DIVORCE. NAME FOUR THINGS YOU COULD DO OR REMEMBER TO HELP YOURSELF FEEL BETTER.

Baseball Situation Cards

YOUR MOM YELLS AT YOU A LOT OF THE TIME. WHAT ARE FOUR THINGS YOU COULD DO TO KEEP HER "OFF YOUR BACK?"

Baseball Situation Cards

YOU MAKE AN **F** ON A MATH TEST. NAME FOUR WAYS YOU COULD IMPROVE YOUR GRADE.

Baseball Situation Cards

YOU DO NOT LIKE THE WAY A FRIEND IS TREATING YOU. NAME FOUR THINGS YOU COULD DO.

Baseball Situation Cards

THE CLASS BULLY KEEPS CALLING YOU NAMES. NAME FOUR WAYS YOU COULD DEAL WITH IT WITHOUT FIGHTING.

Baseball Situation Cards

YOU WOULD REALLY LIKE TO GET ATTENTION FROM YOUR TEACHER. NAME FOUR GOOD WAYS TO GET ATTENTION.

Baseball Situation Cards

YOU WOULD LIKE TO BE SUCCESSFUL. NAME FOUR WAYS TO HELP YOURSELF.

Baseball Situation Cards

YOU WANT TO BE A GOOD FRIEND. NAME FOUR THINGS THAT YOU DEFINITELY SHOULD DO IF YOU WANT TO BE A GOOD FRIEND.

Baseball Situation Cards

NAME FOUR WAYS YOU CAN HELP PEOPLE.

Baseball Situation Cards

YOUR FRIEND SAYS THEY DO
NOT LIKE YOU ANYMORE.
WHAT ARE FOUR THINGS YOU
COULD DO ABOUT IT?

Baseball Situation Cards

YOUR FRIEND'S GRANDFATHER DIED.
WHAT FOUR THINGS COULD YOU DO
TO HELP HIM/HER?

Baseball Situation Cards

YOUR FRIEND IS ALWAYS
TALKING ABOUT HOW DUMB HE/SHE IS.
NAME FOUR POSITIVE THINGS HE/SHE
COULD THINK INSTEAD.

Baseball Situation Cards

YOU WOULD LIKE TO KEEP YOUR TEACHER
"OFF YOUR BACK." WHAT FOUR
THINGS WILL HELP?

Baseball Situation Cards

YOU ARE FEELING SCARED.
WHAT ARE FOUR THINGS
YOU COULD DO?

Baseball Situation Cards

YOU HAVE A FRIEND WHO WANTS TO
STEAL THINGS AT THE MALL. WHAT FOUR
THINGS COULD YOU DO ABOUT
DISCOURAGING THIS?

Baseball Situation Cards

YOU HAVE A FRIEND WHO WANTS
YOU TO SMOKE.
WHAT FOUR RESPONSES
COULD YOU HAVE?

Baseball Situation Cards

YOU FRIEND WANTS TO LIE TO HIS/HER
PARENTS AND YOU DON'T WANT
HIM/HER TO.
WHAT CAN YOU SAY?

CAREER LADDER

Grade Levels: 1-5

Time: 30 Minutes

PURPOSE

To teach children about various careers.

MATERIALS NEEDED

Career Ladder Board
Career Ladder Question Cards
(reproduced & cutout)

OBJECT

To move through the ladder by correctly answering questions to obtain points.

PROCEDURES

1. Divide the class into two groups.

2. Draw a career ladder board. Make six columns and headings for these categories. Make pockets or envelopes in which career ladder questions can be placed. The following categories can be used for the game: training and education, what do they do? what do they need? who would you call? who is it? and to go to college or not? The board would be like the diagram on the next page.

    Behind each 10, 20, 30, 40, and 50 category, a question card is placed in the pocket or envelope. These questions will be worth that number of points, and represent the category under which they have been placed. If more than one game is to be played, you should place more than one set of questions behind each category. To add excitement to the game, place stars on some cards as a bonus (this may be good for extra points as high as 100 or even 500), and make some cards extra turn cards.

Training & education	What do they do?	What do they need?	Who would you call?	Who is it?	To go to college or not?
50	50	50	50	50	50
40	40	40	40	40	40
30	30	30	30	30	30
20	20	20	20	20	20
10	10	10	10	10	10

3. Allow the teams to take turns answering questions. The students must answer the 10 category questions before the 20 category questions and each team can only answer one at a time unless a bonus card is drawn. Keep score of the points for the questions answered.

FOLLOW-UP

Ask the students the following questions:

- What did you learn about careers?

- What standards do most careers have in common for their employees?

- What subjects in school will help get jobs in the future?

TRAINING & EDUCATION
(REQUIRED FOR THE JOB)

What is the training and education required to be a ...

FIREFIGHTER

 **10**

What is the training and education required to be a ...

HAIRDRESSER

 30

What is the training and education required to be a ...

PILOT

 **10**

What is the training and education required to be a ...

COMPUTER PROGRAMMER

 40

What is the training and education required to be a ...

TEACHER

 **20**

What is the training and education required to be a ...

NEWS REPORTER

 **40**

 POWER PLAY

What is the training and education required to be a ...

 LAWYER

What is the training and education required to be a ...

 POLICE OFFICER

What is the training and education required to be a ...

 DOCTOR

What is the training and education required to be a ...

 SECRETARY

WHAT DO THEY DO (IN THEIR JOB)?

What do they do (in their job)?

CONGRESSPERSON

What do they do (in their job)?

RESTAURANT MANAGER

What do they do (in their job)?

ACCOUNTANT

What do they do (in their job)?

COUNSELOR

What do they do (in their job)?

NURSE

What do they do (in their job)?

SECURITY OFFICER

What do they do (in their job)?

SALESPERSON

What do they do (in their job)?

BARBER

What do they do (in their job)?

PARK RANGER

What do they do (in their job)?

WELDER

WHAT DO THEY NEED (FOR THEIR JOB)?

What do they need (for their job)?

LAWYER

10

What do they need (for their job)?

SECRETARY

30

What do they need (for their job)?

FIREFIGHTER

10

What do they need (for their job)?

MUSIC TEACHER

40

What do they need (for their job)?

ENGINEER

20

What do they need (for their job)?

ACCOUNTANT

40

What do they need (for their job)?

ARTIST

20

What do they need (for their job)?

TEACHER

50

What do they need (for their job)?

DOCTOR

30

What do they need (for their job)?

POLICE OFFICER

50

WHO WOULD YOU CALL?

Who would you call...

IF YOUR SINK CLOGS ?

10

Who would you call...

IF YOU NEED A RING MADE ?

20

Who would you call...

IF YOU ARE SICK **?**

Who would you call...

IF YOU NEEDED
A PICTURE MADE **?**

Who would you call...

IF YOU NEEDED HELP
WITH FINDING A BOOK **?**

Who would you call...

IF YOU NEEDED
A HAIRCUT **?**

Who would you call...

IF YOU GOT A BEE STING
AND DIDN'T KNOW
WHAT TO DO **?**

Who would you call...

IF YOUR COMPUTER
WASN'T WORKING **?**

Who would you call...

IF YOU NEED A
WEDDING CAKE MADE **?**

Who would you call...

IF YOU NEED TO OPEN
A CHECKING ACCOUNT **?**

Who would you call...

IF YOU NEED TO
BUY A HOUSE **?**

Who would you call...

IF YOU WANT TO
TALK TO SOMEONE
ABOUT PROBLEMS **?**

Who would you call...

IF YOU NEEDED FOOD
FOR A LOT OF PEOPLE
AT A PARTY**?**

Who would you call...

IF YOU THINK A CHILD
IS BEING HURT**?**

Who would you call...

IF YOU NEED TO FIND
OUT A WAY TO INVENT
A NEW CAR WITH
LOWER GAS MILEAGE **?**

Who would you call...

IF YOU NEED TO
REPORT A ROBBERY **?**

Who would you call...

IF YOU NEED TO FIND
OUT HOW TO
TREAT CANCER **?**

Who would you call...

IF YOU THOUGHT
PEOPLE WERE HUNTING
DEER IN A PLACE
WHERE THEY
SHOULD NOT**?**

WHO IS IT?
(NAME OF THE PERSON
WHO DOES THIS JOB)

Who is...

SOMEONE WHO FLIES AIRPLANES ? **10**

Who is...

SOMEONE WHO ENFORCES THE LAW ? **20**

Who is...

SOMEONE WHO DRIVES A BUS ? **10**

Who is...

SOMEONE WHO HELPS CHILDREN LEARN ? **20**

Who is...

SOMEONE WHO MAKES SURE THE PRISONERS DON'T ESCAPE ? **10**

Who is...

SOMEONE WHO LOOKS AFTER BABIES IN NURSERIES ? **20**

POWER PLAY

Who is...

SOMEONE WHO HELPS ON THE HIGHWAY WITH DRUNK DRIVERS, DRIVERS GOING TOO FAST, AND ACCIDENTS ?

10

Who is...

SOMEONE WHO LOOKS AFTER PEOPLE'S MONEY IN CHECKING AND SAVINGS ACCOUNTS ?

 30

Who is...

SOMEONE WHO FILLS MEDICAL PRESCRIPTIONS ?

 20

Who is...

SOMEONE WHO CUTS MEAT IN THE DELI ?

 30

Who is...

SOMEONE WHO OPERATES ON PEOPLE ?

 30

Who is...

SOMEONE WHO REPAIRS COMMODES AND SINKS ?

40

Who is...

SOMEONE WHO MAKES RINGS ?

 30

Who is...

SOMEONE WHO BUILDS ROADS ?

 50

Who is...

SOMEONE WHO GIVES SERMONS ON SUNDAY MORNINGS AND HELPS PEOPLE ?

Who is...

SOMEONE WHO BUILDS BUILDINGS ?

Who is...

SOMEONE WHO WORKS IN THE YARD ?

Who is...

SOMEONE WHO CEMENTS BRICKS TOGETHER ON HOUSES ?

Who is...

SOMEONE WHO WORKS IN THEIR STATE CAPITOL OR WASHINGTON, DC AND HELPS MAKE LAWS ?

Who is...

SOMEONE WHO TAKES MONEY AT BANKS AND MAKES DEPOSITS TO ACCOUNTS ?

Who is...

SOMEONE WHO RINGS UP YOUR GROCERIES?

Who is...

SOMEONE WHO FIXES YOUR CAR?

To Go to College or Not?

Do you need a college education to be a...

Teacher ?

Do you need a college education to be a...

Store Clerk ?

Do you need a college education to be a...

Taxi Driver ?

Do you need a college education to be a...

Factory Worker ?

Do you need a college education to be a...

Doctor ?

Do you need a college education to be a...

Counselor ?

Do you need a college education to be a...

Receptionist ?

Do you need a college education to be a...

Lawyer ?

Do you need a college education to be a...

LANDSCAPER **?**

Do you need a college education to be a...

ROCKET SCIENTIST **?**

Do you need a college education to be a...

X-RAY TECHNICIAN **?**

Do you need a college education to be a...

LAB TECHNICIAN **?**

Do you need a college education to be a...

PILOT **?**

Do you need a college education to be a...

SOCIAL WORKER **?**

Do you need a college education to be a...

POSTAL WORKER **?**

Do you need a college education to be a...

MCDONALD'S CLERK **?**

118

Do you need a college education to be a...

POLICE OFFICER ?

Do you need a college education to be a...

SECRETARY ?

Do you need a college education to be a...

ACCOUNTANT ?

Do you need a college education to be a...

ADVERTISING SALESPERSON ?

Do you need a college education to be a...

DENTIST ?

Do you need a college education to be a...

STORE OWNER ?

Do you need a college education to be a...

ELECTRICIAN ?

Do you need a college education to be a...

COSMETOLOGIST ?

Section III:

Social Skills

Sometimes, educators take it for granted that appropriate social skills have already been taught and practiced in the home. However, this may not always be the case. Children's social skills are influenced by TV, movies, videos, books and music lyrics. Many social interactions children view or hear through the media are not acceptable methods of social interactions appropriate to use with their peers and with adults.

Inappropriate social skills not only get a student in trouble with teachers and administrators, but also receive negative reactions from other students. Therefore, the teaching of appropriate social skills is necessary to help provide an ongoing awareness of appropriate interaction in social situations. Learning these skills through games provides not only a fun format, but also teaches appropriate manners, respectful attitudes, and polite responses to a variety of situations that students face on a daily basis.

LINE IT UP

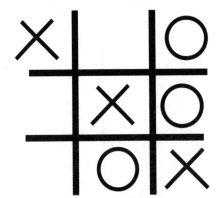

Grade Levels: 1-5

Time: 30 Minutes

PURPOSE
To teach students acceptable ways of dealing with social situations.

MATERIALS NEEDED
Line It Up Cards (reproduced & cutout)
Nine chairs
Five X cards
Five O cards

OBJECT
To form a Tic-Tac-Toe before the other team by answering questions appropriately.

PROCEDURES

1. Set up three rows of three chairs in a central location in the classroom.

2. Make five cards with an X on them and five with an O on them.

3. Line It Up Problem Cards contain questions describing various social situations in which the students might find themselves. Mix the cards.

4. Divide students into two teams. Ask teams to choose either the X's or the O's then give them the appropriate cards.

5. Choose one student to start. This student chooses a Line It Up Problem Card, and you read the question. Determine if the answer is appropriate. If the student gets the question right, ask the student to choose a chair and sit on it while holding either their X or O card.

6. Play goes to the other team.

7. Play continues until one team has Tic-Tac-Toe.

VARIATIONS

- Questions can be changed according to problems arising in the classroom. Questions may also be directed towards the curriculum, areas which involve interpersonal conflict in particular. Using curriculum questions, students can not only cover subject matter, but also be given the opportunity to brainstorm solutions to interpersonal problems.

- The Tic-Tac-Toe diagram may be put on the board and the student may write in their team's X or O if the question is answered correctly.

FOLLOW-UP

Focus discussion on what students learned from answering the questions, and ask how these situations can be integrated into the classroom. You can encourage students to work on implementing the strategies, and give verbal reinforcement when a student does implement a particular strategy.

Line It Up Problem Cards

Line It Up Problem Cards

WHAT WOULD YOU DO IF SOMEONE ASKED YOU TO RIDE HOME WITH THEM AND YOU DIDN'T KNOW THEM?

Line It Up Problem Cards

HOW DO YOU DEAL WITH SAD FEELINGS?

Line It Up Problem Cards

HOW WOULD YOU INTRODUCE SOMEONE TO SOMEONE ELSE?

Line It Up Problem Cards

HOW DO YOU DEAL WITH A PARENT'S DIVORCE?

Line It Up Problem Cards

SHOW HOW YOUR BODY WOULD BE POSITIONED IF YOU WERE PAYING ATTENTION.

Line It Up Problem Cards

HOW DO YOU DEAL WITH MAD FEELINGS?

Line It Up Problem Cards

HOW DO YOU STUDY FOR A TEST?

Line It Up Problem Cards

WHAT DO YOU DO IF SOMEONE TOUCHES YOU INAPPROPRIATELY?

Line It Up Problem Cards

HOW DO YOU SOLVE A PROBLEM?

Line It Up Problem Cards

WHAT DO YOU DO IF YOUR BABYSITTER IS LETTING YOU WATCH R-RATED MOVIES?

Line It Up Problem Cards

WHAT DO YOU DO IF YOUR BEST FRIEND DOESN'T CALL YOU ANYMORE?

Line It Up Problem Cards

WHAT DO YOU DO IF YOUR BEST FRIEND WANTS TO TRY DRUGS?

Line It Up Problem Cards

WHAT DO YOU DO IF SOMEONE WON'T SPEAK TO YOU AND YOU DON'T KNOW WHY?

Line It Up Problem Cards

WHAT THINGS DO YOU NEED TO DO IN THE CLASSROOM TO SUCCEED?

Line It Up Problem Cards

WHAT DO YOU DO IF SOMEONE'S GRANDMOTHER DIES?

Line It Up Problem Cards

HOW DO YOU MAKE NEW FRIENDS?

Line It Up Problem Cards

WHAT DO YOU DO IF YOUR GRADES ARE DROPPING?

Line It Up Problem Cards

WHAT WOULD YOU DO IF YOUR BEST FRIEND STARTED TALKING ABOUT EVERYONE IN A BAD WAY?

Line It Up Problem Cards

WHAT DO YOU DO IF YOU ARE HAVING A PROBLEM WITH A FRIEND?

Line It Up Problem Cards

WHAT DO YOU DO IF YOU ARE NOT HAPPY AT HOME?

Line It Up Problem Cards

WHAT DO YOU DO IF YOU'RE HAVING DIFFICULTY IGNORING WHAT OTHERS SAY TO YOU?

Line It Up Problem Cards

WHAT DO YOU DO IF YOUR BROTHER OR SISTER KEEPS BEATING ON YOU?

Line It Up Problem Cards

WHAT DO YOU DO IF YOU ARE NOT HAPPY AT SCHOOL?

Line It Up Problem Cards

WHAT WOULD YOU DO IF A FRIEND WANTS YOU TO TAKE A CIGARETTE OR SOME BEER?

WHO DO YOU THINK YOU'RE TALKING TO?

Grade Levels: 2-Middle School

Time: 30 Minutes

PURPOSE

To help students learn the difference between expressing themselves in an acceptable and unacceptable way through tone of voice and body language.

MATERIALS NEEDED

People Cards (reproduced & cutout)
Sentence Feeling Cards (reproduced & cutout)
Two identical clown faces
Construction paper facial features
(reproduced & cutout)

OBJECT

To complete the clown face before the other team by responding appropriately to questions and situations.

PROCEDURES

1. Divide the students into two teams.

2. Ask one team member to choose a People Card and a Sentence Feeling Card. The People Card contains names of persons you could say things to. These names represent authority figures as well as non-authority figures. The Sentence Feeling Card contains a sentence that could be said in two tones of voice or using two types of emotion.

3. Ask the team member to choose the correct tone and exhibit the appropriate body language which would be all right to use with the name on the People Card. For example, if a People Card has "Teacher" on it and the Sentence Feeling Card says "Oh, no." (angry or excited), In order to be using the appropriate tone, a student needs to choose the excited tone and not the angry tone.

4. The team earns a point if the team member chooses the appropriate tone of voice, then answers the People card using the appropriate body language and tone of voice.

5. When a point is earned, a part for the team's clown face is added to a clown picture.

6. The team that adds the most parts to the clown wins.

VARIATION

Let each team member draw the clown parts to an oval face on the board. For example, using chalk they could add a hat, nose, eyes, mouth, etc. for each correct response.

FOLLOW-UP

Ask the students the following questions:

- What tone and body language did you enjoy using the most?

- Does the body language and tone make a difference to the person with whom you are speaking? How?

- How would it help you to use the appropriate body language and tone with others?

Sentence Feeling Cards

Sentence Feeling Cards

"I'm going home."
(happy, sad)

Sentence Feeling Cards

"I have a baby sister."
(jealous, happy)

Sentence Feeling Cards

"Oh, no."
(angry, excited)

Sentence Feeling Cards

"Our neighbor has
a big police dog."
(afraid, curious)

Sentence Feeling Cards

"Our class is
going to P.E."
(upset, confused)

Sentence Feeling Cards

"I'm going to school."
(upset, curious)

Sentence Feeling Cards

"My uncle sent
me $100."
(proud, lonely)

Sentence Feeling Cards

"I'm going to sit down."
(surprised, annoyed)

Sentence Feeling Cards

"I didn't do
my homework."
(afraid, proud)

Sentence Feeling Cards

"Give me a pencil."
(angry, surprised)

Sentence Feeling Cards

"I didn't do it."
(angry, humble)

Sentence Feeling Cards

"She hit me."
(teasing, assertive)

Sentence Feeling Cards

"I'm sorry I
bumped you."
(sarcastic, apologetic)

Sentence Feeling Cards

"Did you call me?"
(threatening, happily)

Sentence Feeling Cards

"I can't do my
homework."
(angry, depressed)

Sentence Feeling Cards

"Stop joking around."
(jokingly, sadly)

CLOWN FACES

POWER PLAY

POWER PLAY

Clown Face Parts

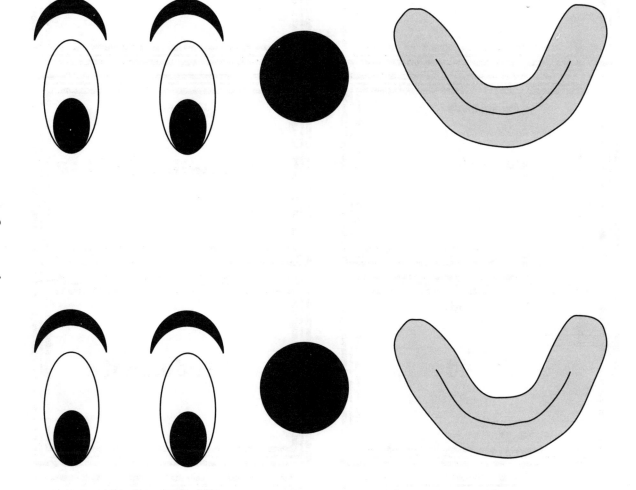

PEOPLE CARDS
(IMPORTANT TO USE CORRECT TONE)

People Cards

Teacher

People Cards

Parent

People Cards

Preacher

People Cards

A smaller child

People Cards

Friend

People Cards

Grandparent

People Cards

Baby

People Cards

Enemy

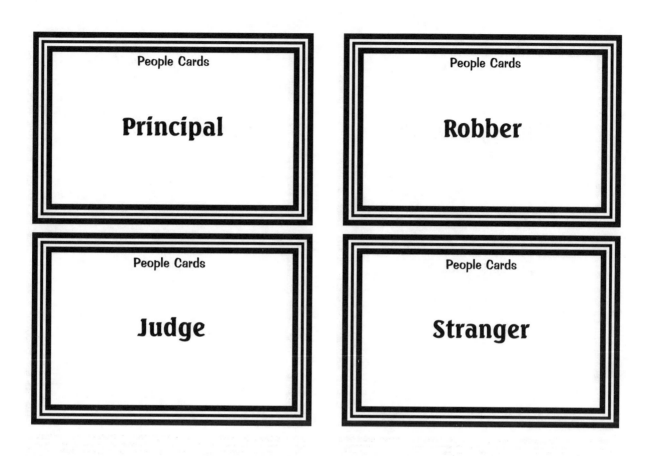

People Cards

Principal

People Cards

Robber

People Cards

Judge

People Cards

Stranger

PEOPLE CARDS
(TONE USED MAKES NO DIFFERENCE)

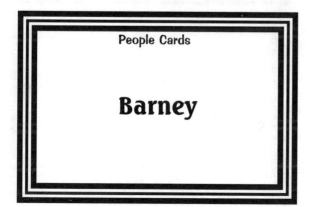

People Cards

Barney

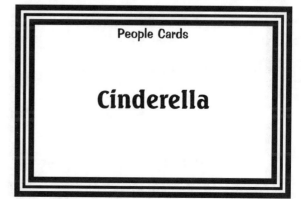

People Cards

Cinderella

People Cards

Mickey Mouse

People Cards

Cookie Monster

People Cards

Monster

People Cards

Big Bird

People Cards

Clown

People Cards

Bugs Bunny

People Cards

Vampire

People Cards

Snow White

POWER PLAY

People Cards

Ghost

People Cards

Dumbo

POWER PLAY

YES OR NO GAME

Grade Levels: 1-5   **Time: 30 Minutes**

PURPOSE

To identify behaviors that indicate good social skills.

MATERIALS NEEDED

Yes or No Situation Cards (reproduced & cutout)
Yes or No Cards (reproduced on different color
paper & cutout)
Yes or No game board
Colored cards

OBJECT

TO GET THREE ROWS OF SIX YES ANSWERS OR NO
ANSWERS IN A ROW, EITHER VERTICALLY,
HORIZONTALLY, OR DIAGONALLY.

PROCEDURES

1. Make a large game board on a sheet of poster board with six boxes across and six boxes down.

2. Make a pocket by stapling an index card or piece of paper inside each box big enough to hold one question.

3. Put a Yes or No card in each pocket.

4. Since the object of the game will be to get six yes answers or no answers in a row either vertically, horizontally, or diagonally, questions will need to be strategically placed. Place at least three rows of yes or no answers. (Please note diagram on page 138 showing three rows of no questions. The positions of the three rows can be changed.) All questions must be hidden

POWER PLAY

in pockets or turned around. The game is won when all three rows are found. (Note: you must know the location of the patterns. The students will have to discover the patterns.)

5.   Make two different colors of cards to be placed in the pockets with the Yes or No Cards. One color signifies yes answers and the other color signifies no answers. Place the appropriate card in each pocket after the question has been answered.

6.   To begin play, ask a student to come up and choose a card and answer the card. Ask him/her to place the corresponding colored card in the pocket to indicate the correct answer to the question.

7.   Ask students to look for patterns across the board.

8.   Play continues until game is won by finding all three rows of yes or no answers.

9.   Note the three patterns found in the example on page 138. The first is found in the first row in a horizontal pattern. The second is found in the fifth box in a vertical pattern. The third is found in the sixth box in a diagonal pattern going down to the left. Sporadically place other questions. Students must discover the patterns.

FOLLOW-UP

Focus discussion on helping students learn positive behaviors to help them grow socially, emotionally, and academically. Continually pointing out the pluses of this behavior may help bring these positive behaviors into a student's quality world. Such behavior will enable students to feel more successful both personally and academically. Any means of reinforcement of positive work habits is certainly of benefit.

Yes or No Game Board

Should I lie to my teacher? **NO**	Should I sing in the cafeteria while everyone else is quiet? **NO**	Should I hit my friend in the head? **NO**	Should I gossip about my friends? **NO**	Should I allow a kid to make me do something I don't want to? **NO**	Should I call people stupid? **NO**
Should I be nice to people regardless of their race? **YES**	Should I try to do my best on my school work? **YES**	Should I listen to my teacher during math? **YES**	Should I be polite to my mom? **YES**	Should I pinch somebody in the arm? **NO**	Should I give compliments to my friends? **YES**
Should I clean up my desk for my teacher? **YES**	Should I keep myself clean? **YES**	Should I drink beer with all my friends? **NO**	Should I stand on my desk? **NO**	Should I throw a fit in the store? **NO**	Should I be respectful of adults? **YES**
Should I ask people nicely to leave me alone when I don't like what they're doing? **YES**	Should I talk about my feelings when I'm sad? **YES**	Should I steal from my friends? **NO**	Should I be loyal to my friends? **YES**	Should I goof off in class? **NO**	Should I walk away from people if they are doing things I don't agree with? **YES**
Should I play hooky from school? **NO**	Should I do drugs? **NO**	Should I talk to a trusted adult about my problems? **YES**	Should I eat healthy foods? **YES**	Should I assault anyone? **NO**	Should I bring my homework to school? **YES**
Should I ride with strangers? **NO**	Should I eat ten candy bars per day? **NO**	Should I talk about my feelings when I'm happy? **YES**	Should I ignore people at times when they bother me? **YES**	Should I bring knives and guns to school? **NO**	Should I go to the park without my teacher's permission? **NO**

YES OR NO SITUATION CARDS

© 1997 by YouthLight, Inc.

Yes or No Situation Cards

SHOULD I LIE TO MY TEACHER?

Yes or No Situation Cards

SHOULD I BE NICE TO PEOPLE REGARDLESS OF THEIR RACE?

Yes or No Situation Cards

SHOULD I CLEAN UP MY DESK FOR MY TEACHER?

Yes or No Situation Cards

SHOULD I SING IN THE CAFETERIA WHILE EVERYONE ELSE IS QUIET?

Yes or No Situation Cards

SHOULD I HIT MY FRIEND IN THE HEAD?

Yes or No Situation Cards

SHOULD I TRY TO DO MY BEST ON MY SCHOOL WORK?

Yes or No Situation Cards

SHOULD I GOSSIP ABOUT MY FRIENDS?

Yes or No Situation Cards

SHOULD I LISTEN TO MY TEACHER DURING MATH?

Yes or No Situation Cards **SHOULD I BE POLITE TO MY MOM?**	Yes or No Situation Cards **SHOULD I PINCH SOMEBODY ON THE ARM?**
Yes or No Situation Cards **SHOULD I GIVE COMPLIMENTS TO MY FRIENDS?**	Yes or No Situation Cards **SHOULD I STAND ON MY DESK?**
Yes or No Situation Cards **SHOULD I THROW A FIT IN THE STORE?**	Yes or No Situation Cards **SHOULD I GOOF OFF IN CLASS?**
Yes or No Situation Cards **SHOULD I KEEP MYSELF CLEAN?**	Yes or No Situation Cards **SHOULD I DRINK BEER WITH ALL MY FRIENDS?**

© 1997 by YouthLight, Inc.

Yes or No Situation Cards

SHOULD I BE
RESPECTFUL OF ADULTS?

Yes or No Situation Cards

SHOULD I ASK PEOPLE NICELY
TO LEAVE ME ALONE WHEN I
DON'T LIKE WHAT THEY'RE
DOING?

Yes or No Situation Cards

SHOULD I STEAL
FROM MY FRIENDS?

Yes or No Situation Cards

SHOULD I TALK ABOUT
MY FEELINGS WHEN I'M SAD?

Yes or No Situation Cards

SHOULD I BE LOYAL
TO MY FRIENDS?

Yes or No Situation Cards

SHOULD I WALK AWAY FROM
PEOPLE IF THEY ARE DOING
THINGS I DON'T AGREE WITH?

Yes or No Situation Cards

SHOULD I PLAY
HOOKY FROM SCHOOL?

Yes or No Situation Cards

SHOULD I EAT
HEALTHY FOODS?

142

Yes or No Situation Cards

SHOULD I BRING MY HOMEWORK TO SCHOOL?

Yes or No Situation Cards

SHOULD I ASSAULT ANYONE?

Yes or No Situation Cards

SHOULD I RIDE WITH STRANGERS?

Yes or No Situation Cards

SHOULD I EAT TEN CANDY BARS PER DAY?

Yes or No Situation Cards

SHOULD I TALK ABOUT MY FEELINGS WHEN I'M HAPPY?

Yes or No Situation Cards

SHOULD I IGNORE PEOPLE AT TIMES WHEN THEY BOTHER ME?

Yes or No Situation Cards

SHOULD I BRING KNIVES AND GUNS TO SCHOOL?

Yes or No Situation Cards

SHOULD I GO TO THE PARK WITHOUT MY TEACHER'S PERMISSION?

Yes or No Situation Cards

SHOULD I ASK SOMEONE TO STOP IF I DON'T LIKE THE WAY THEY ARE TOUCHING ME?

Yes or No Situation Cards

SHOULD I NEVER STUDY FOR TEST?

Yes or No Situation Cards

SHOULD I ALLOW A KID TO MAKE ME DO SOMETHING I DON'T WANT TO?

Yes or No Situation Cards

SHOULD I CALL PEOPLE STUPID?

Yes or No Situation Cards

SHOULD I HELP MY FRIENDS WHEN THEY NEED ME?

Yes or No Situation Cards

SHOULD I STEAL JUST FOR THE FUN OF IT?

YES OR NO CARDS

YES

YES

144

YES

YES

YES

YES

YES

YES

YES

YES

© 1997 by YouthLight, Inc.

POWER PLAY

YES

YES

YES

YES

YES

YES

YES

YES

Power Play

YES

YES

NO

NO

NO

NO

NO

NO

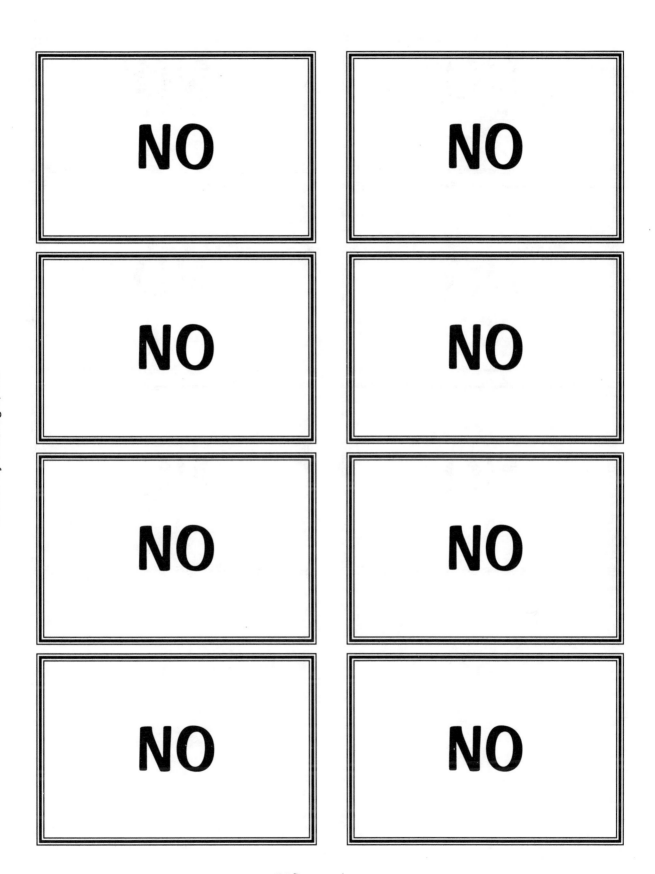

NO

NO

NO

NO

NO

NO

CATCH A CARP
(GAME 1)

Grade Levels: K-3

Time: 40 Minutes

PURPOSE
To teach students appropriate means of dealing with social situations.

MATERIALS NEEDED
Catch a Carp Question Cards
(reproduced & cutout)
Fishing pond (made out of construction paper)
List of questions
Stick for fishing pole
Metal paper clips or magnets
Magnet for fishing pole

OBJECT
To catch the most fish.

PROCEDURES

1. Make a "pond" (about three feet by three feet) to be placed on the floor.

2. Lay the Catch a Carp Question Cards face down in the pond. Place a star on some "fish" to signify that the student who chooses that particular fish gets a prize. Place a symbol on one or two fish to signify that everyone gets a prize. Attach magnets or paper clips to all Catch a Carp Question Cards.

3. Make a fishing pole with a magnet attached to a string on the end of the pole.

4. Ask students to take turns going fishing. Each child goes fishing by throwing the fishing pole in the fishing pond and catching a fish. Ask the child to answer the question which corresponds with the number.

5. Play continues until time runs out or until each child has had a turn.

CATCH A CARP
(GAME 2)

MATERIALS NEEDED

Catch a Carp Question & Answer Cards
(reproduced & cutout)
Fishing pond (made out of construction paper)
List of questions
Stick for fishing pole
Metal paper clips or magnets
Magnet for fishing pole

Objects

To get the most points.
or
To get 100 points first.

PROCEDURES

1. Make two fishing ponds, one containing "problem fish," and one containing "answer fish." this becomes a matching and concentration game. Again, the problems are social skills questions.

2. Divide the class into two teams.

3. Choose one person to begin and go fishing for a problem fish. Then give the team three chances to go fishing in the answer pond to come up with an appropriate solution to the problem. If the team can appropriately justify a particular response, it is counted as a match. Each match awards 10 points to the team. The answers they do not use must be put back in the pond.

4. If a team does not get an appropriate response in their three chances, they can hold the problem fish until next time. Hopefully, by paying attention, they may see the other team turn over an appropriate answer.

5. Play continues until one team gets 100 points, until both teams get 50 points, or until time runs out.

VARIATION

Divide the class into teams and place point values on every fish. Not only can the students answer the questions, but they can see which team accumulates the most points. To get the points, the question must be answered appropriately.

FOLLOW-UP

- Focus discussion on various situations found on the Catch a Carp Cards and how students might implement one strategy learned during the next week.

- You could make a bulletin board with fish on the board. Whenever students implemented a strategy, their name and successful behavior could be written on the board. This would reinforce positive behaviors noted during the week.

Catch a Carp Social Skills Question List

> Note: Some questions are of a very serious nature. Please use your own judgement in administering the game using these questions. However, these questions may give you a good opportunity to bring up appropriate behavior in tough situations without going into lots of detail, using a non-threatening manner.

1. What would you say if your friend seemed very sad and didn't want to play with you?

2. What would you say if your friend didn't invite you to their party and invited your other friends?

3. What would you say if your friend had something you wanted to play with?

4. What would you say if your friend didn't bring back something they borrowed from you?

5. What would you say if your friend said your shoes looked stupid?

6. What would you say if your friend wanted you to go somewhere your mom said you couldn't go?

7. What would you say if your friend wanted you to smoke a cigarette for fun?

8. What would you say if your friend wanted to copy your paper?

9. What would you say if your friend wanted to leave someone out of a group activity?

10. What would you say if your friend wanted to go to the R-rated movie when your mom thought you were at a G-rated movie?

11. What would you say if your friend wanted you to steal a piece of bubble gum at the store just to see if you could?

12. What would you say if your friend wanted to try some beer and wanted you to do the same?

13. What would you say if your friend threatened to hit you?

14. What would you say if your friend was getting on your nerves?

15. What would you say if your friend kept getting in trouble?

16. What would you say if your friend never brought in their homework and told you that you were a nerd if you did?

17. What would you say if your friend wanted you to cheat on a test?

18. What would you say if your friend wanted you to help them beat someone up?

19. What would you say if someone kept calling you a jerk?

20. What would you say if someone kept calling you stupid?

21. What would you say if someone kept tapping on your desk?

22. What would say if someone kept putting their hands all over your stuff?

23. What would you say if someone kept staring at you?

24. What would you say if someone kept looking at your paper in math?

25. What would you say if someone kept threatening you?

26. What would you say if an adult kept hitting and bruising you?

27. What would you do if an adult made you feel uncomfortable by the way they touched you?

28. What would you say if a stranger wanted you to go with them to find your mom?

29. What would you say if a child touched you a in a way you didn't like?

30. What would you say if you got lost in the mall?

CATCH A CARP QUESTION CARDS

What would you say if...

YOUR FRIEND SEEMED VERY
SAD AND DIDN'T WANT TO
PLAY WITH YOU?

1

Catch a Carp Question Cards

What would you say if...

YOUR FRIEND DIDN'T INVITE YOU
TO THEIR PARTY AND INVITED
YOUR OTHER FRIENDS?

2

Catch a Carp Question Cards

What would you say if...

YOUR FRIEND HAD
SOMETHING YOU WANTED
TO PLAY WITH?

3

Catch a Carp Question Cards

What would you say if...

YOUR FRIEND DIDN'T BRING
BACK SOMETHING THEY
BORROWED FROM YOU?

4

Catch a Carp Question Cards

What would you say if...

YOUR FRIEND SAID
YOUR SHOES
LOOKED STUPID?

5

Catch a Carp Question Cards

What would you say if...

YOUR FRIEND WANTED
YOU TO GO SOMEWHERE YOUR
MOM SAID YOU COULDN'T GO?

6

Catch a Carp Question Cards

What would you say if...

YOUR FRIEND WANTED
YOU TO SMOKE A
CIGARETTE FOR FUN?

7

Catch a Carp Question Cards

What would you say if...

YOUR FRIEND WANTED
TO COPY YOUR PAPER?

8

Catch a Carp Question Cards

© 1997 by YouthLight, Inc.

POWER PLAY

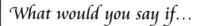

What would you say if…

YOUR FRIEND WANTED TO
LEAVE SOMEONE OUT OF
A GROUP ACTIVITY?

9

Catch a Carp Question Cards

What would you say if…

YOUR FRIEND WANTED TO GO TO
THE R-RATED MOVIE WHEN
YOUR MOM THOUGHT YOU
WERE AT A G-RATED MOVIE?

10

Catch a Carp Question Cards

What would you say if…

YOUR FRIEND WANTED YOU
TO STEAL A PIECE OF BUBBLE GUM
AT THE STORE JUST TO SEE
IF YOU COULD?

11

Catch a Carp Question Cards

What would you say if…

YOUR FRIEND WANTED TO TRY
SOME BEER AND WANTED
YOU TO DO THE SAME?

12

Catch a Carp Question Cards

What would you say if…

YOUR FRIEND THREATENED
TO HIT YOU?

13

Catch a Carp Question Cards

What would you say if…

YOUR FRIEND WAS GETTING
ON YOUR NERVES?

14

Catch a Carp Question Cards

What would you say if…

YOUR FRIEND KEPT
GETTING IN TROUBLE?

15

Catch a Carp Question Cards

What would you say if…

YOUR FRIEND NEVER BROUGHT
IN THEIR HOMEWORK AND
TOLD YOU THAT YOU WERE A NERD
IF YOU DID?

16

Catch a Carp Question Cards

What would you say if…

YOUR FRIEND WANTED
YOU TO CHEAT ON A TEST?

17

Catch a Carp Question Cards

What would you say if…

YOUR FRIENDS WANTED YOU TO
HELP THEM BEAT SOMEONE UP?

18

Catch a Carp Question Cards

What would you say if…

SOMEONE KEPT CALLING
YOU A JERK?

19

Catch a Carp Question Cards

What would you say if…

SOMEONE KEPT CALLING
YOU STUPID?

20

Catch a Carp Question Cards

What would you say if…

SOMEONE KEPT TAPPING
ON YOUR DESK?

21

Catch a Carp Question Cards

What would you say if…

SOMEONE KEPT PUTTING
THEIR HANDS ALL
OVER YOUR STUFF?

22

Catch a Carp Question Cards

What would you say if…

SOMEONE KEPT STARING
AT YOU?

23

Catch a Carp Question Cards

What would you say if…

SOMEONE KEPT LOOKING
AT YOUR PAPER IN MATH?

24

Catch a Carp Question Cards

What would you say if…

SOMEONE KEPT THREATENING YOU?

25
Catch a Carp Question Cards

What would you say if…

AN ADULT KEPT HITTING AND BRUISING YOU?

26
Catch a Carp Question Cards

What would you say if…

AN ADULT MADE YOU FEEL UNCOMFORTABLE BY THE WAY THEY TOUCHED YOU?

27
Catch a Carp Question Cards

What would you say if…

A STRANGER WANTED YOU TO GO WITH THEM TO FIND YOUR MOM?

28
Catch a Carp Question Cards

What would you say if…

A CHILD TOUCHED YOU IN A WAY YOU DIDN'T LIKE?

29
Catch a Carp Question Cards

What would you say if…

YOU GOT LOST AT A MALL?

30
Catch a Carp Question Cards

POWER PLAY

CATCH A CARP ANSWER CARDS

Note: If you are playing game two, the following answers may be added to the answer pond. Use only twenty questions because this game may take a longer time. Match these answers with the questions on pages 154 through 157.

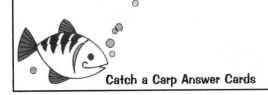

"WHY ARE YOU SO SAD TODAY? WOULD YOU LIKE TO TALK?"

Catch a Carp Answer Cards

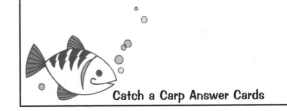

"NO THANKS, I DON'T WANT TO GO. I HAVE SOMEWHERE ELSE TO BE."

Catch a Carp Answer Cards

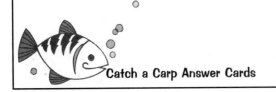

"NOT ME MAN - I'M NOT GETTING IN TROUBLE."

Catch a Carp Answer Cards

"I WILL GO PLAY WITH SOMEONE ELSE."

Catch a Carp Answer Cards

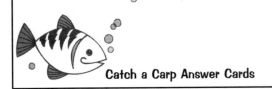

"NO THANKS, I DON'T SMOKE."

Catch a Carp Answer Cards

"NO, THAT'S NOT COOL! I'VE HEARD IT KILLS BRAIN CELLS, AND I NEED ALL I CAN GET."

Catch a Carp Answer Cards

POWER PLAY

"MAY I PLEASE
PLAY WITH THAT?"

Catch a Carp Answer Cards

"I'M GOING TO COVER
MY PAPER BECAUSE THE
TEACHER LIKES US TO DO THAT."

Catch a Carp Answer Cards

"MAN, LEAVE ME ALONE - YOU
KNOW WE'LL BOTH MISS
RECESS IF YOU KEEP IT UP."

Catch a Carp Answer Cards

"COULD YOU PLEASE
BRING IT BACK? IF NOT, COULD YOU
BRING ME A NEW ONE?"

Catch a Carp Answer Cards

"SAY, SHE'S PRETTY FUN,
LET'S PLAY WITH HER."

Catch a Carp Answer Cards

"THANK YOU FOR NOTICING,
BUT I REALLY LIKE MY SHOES."

Catch a Carp Answer Cards

"SAY MAN, WHY DON'T YOU
QUIT GETTING IN TROUBLE. I
MISS YOU WHEN YOU CAN'T
GO OUTSIDE WITH ME."

Catch a Carp Answer Cards

"NOT ME - I'M NOT CHEATING -
MAKING AN O IS A LOT WORSE GRADE
THAN IF I DO SOMETHING ON MY OWN."

Catch a Carp Answer Cards

POWER PLAY

"I BELIEVE I WILL IGNORE
THAT LAST RIDICULOUS COMMENT
SINCE IT COULDN'T POSSIBLY
APPLY TO ME."

Catch a Carp Answer Cards

"SAY MAN - I'M DOING MY
HOMEWORK - OTHERWISE I'LL FAIL.
I DON'T KNOW ABOUT YOU, BUT MY
FUTURE HOUSING PLANS DON'T INCLUDE
THE HOMELESS SHELTER."

Catch a Carp Answer Cards

"NOT ME - I DON'T HAVE
ANY BANDAGES FOR MY
KNUCKLES - ANYWAY, I DON'T
LIKE THE SIGHT OF BLOOD."

Catch a Carp Answer Cards

"STUPID - ME? THAT HARDLY
APPLIES TO A GENIUS LIKE ME - YOU
MUST BE MISTAKEN."

Catch a Carp Answer Cards

"MAN, I REALLY WANTED
TO SEE THAT OTHER MOVIE.
I THINK I'LL GO TO THAT ONE."

Catch a Carp Answer Cards

"CHILL OUT - LEAVE ME ALONE!"

Catch a Carp Answer Cards

"I'LL TELL SOMEONE I TRUST."

Catch a Carp Answer Cards

"NOT ME MAN - I DON'T PICK
ON KIDS LIKE THAT!"

Catch a Carp Answer Cards

"Do I look that good? Thanks!"

Catch a Carp Answer Cards

"I don't like this! Stop it!"

Catch a Carp Answer Cards

"I know you're not talking to me."

Catch a Carp Answer Cards

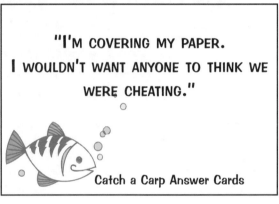

"I'm covering my paper. I wouldn't want anyone to think we were cheating."

Catch a Carp Answer Cards

MILLIONAIRE MESSAGES

Grade Levels: 3-5

Time: 30 Minutes

PURPOSE

To familiarize students with lessons in life skills as taught
by old adages and proverbs.

MATERIALS NEEDED

Proverb Cards (reproduced & cutout)
Proverb Meaning Cards (reproduced & cutout)
List of proverbs
List of proverb meanings
Play money

OBJECT

For one group to match
the proverb meanings with
the correct proverb.

Procedures

1.   Define proverbs as short sayings that have a well-known truth, to the class or group.

2.   Divide the students into two groups.

3.   Pass out a Proverb Card to each member of one group. Pass out a Proverb Meaning Card to
     each member of the other group.

4.   Ask the group with the Proverb Cards to read them aloud with each member taking a turn.

5.   Once the proverb has been read, the student with the matching Proverb Meaning Card goes
     to stand behind the proverb student whom they think they match. Alternatively, students may
     raise their hands when they have found their match.

6. If they are correct, the person with the correct matching meaning gets one million dollars play money.

7. Give a bonus of one dollar if the student with the Proverb Meaning Card can say the Proverb from memory.

8. Switch the groups to allow the previous proverb readers to earn money.

9. The group with the most money wins. (Millionaire = rich in good lessons or messages.)

VARIATION

The person reading the proverbs also gets one million dollars if he/she can determine if the meaning student has a correct match instead of the leader doing this. The proverb student could also win one bonus dollar if the proverb can be stated from memory.

FOLLOW-UP

Ask the students the following questions:

- What proverb lesson was a good one for you to remember? Why?

- What made it easy for you to make a match?

- What made it hard for you to make a match?

- Could these lessons in life be helpful to you in your life? How?

- With which proverbs do you agree or disagree? Why?

PROVERBS

Note: The numbers on the Proverb Cards correspond to the matching Proverb Meaning Card.

Proverbs

Nothing ventured,
nothing gained.

1

Proverbs

Beauty is only
skin deep.

2

Proverbs

One rotten apple
spoils the whole barrel.

3

Proverbs

Actions speak louder
than words.

4

Proverbs

Every cloud has
a silver lining.

5

Proverbs

A word to the
wise is sufficient.

6

Proverbs

If at first you don't
succeed, try, try again.

7

Proverbs

Fools rush in where
angels fear to tread.

8

Proverbs

Never put off until
tomorrow what you
can do today.

9

Proverbs

Two heads are
better than one.

10

Proverbs

Necessity is the
mother of invention.

11

Proverbs

Make hay while
the sun shines.

12

PROVERB MEANINGS

| Note: The numbers on the Proverb Meaning Cards correspond to the matching Proverb Card. |

Proverb Meanings

You won't know if you
can do something
unless you try.

1

Proverb Meanings

Being a nice person is more
important than
being pretty.

2

Proverb Meanings

If someone is
not good, it messes
up the whole group.

3

Proverb Meanings

It is more important
to do what needs to
be done rather than
talk about it.

4

Proverb Meanings

Even good can come
out of sad or bad things
happening to you.

5

Proverb Meanings

If you are smart, you will
listen to good advise.

6

Proverb Meanings

Keep trying and don't
give up even when
it is hard.

7

Proverb Meanings

Don't be foolish by
doing things that good smart
folks wouldn't.

8

Proverb Meanings

Do now what needs
to be done. Don't wait
to do things.

9

Proverb Meanings

You can work things out
better with a partner.

10

Proverb Meanings

You come up with an answer
to a problem when you need it.

11

Proverb Meanings

Do as much work as you can
while you have time.

12

MANNERS MATTER

Grade Levels: K-4

Time: 30 Minutes

PURPOSE

To teach students the importance of having good manners.

MATERIALS NEEDED

Manners Cards (reproduced & cutout)
Laminated circles or squares

OBJECT

To acquire the most points for
your team by drawing cards that move
the player to the finish line.

PROCEDURES

1. Divide the class into two teams.

2. Put down equal number of laminated circles or squares in two separate lines on the floor. Begin with ten to fifteen circles in each line.

3. Put a list of Manners Cards in a central location. Each Manners Card has a plus sign and a number, or a minus sign and a number. The plus numbers indicate good manners (helping the teacher, +4) and the minus signs indicate bad manners (burping, -2).

4. Choose two students to play the game, one from each team. The object will be to see who will be able to get across the circles or squares the fastest.

5. The first student stands at the beginning of one row and asks someone from his/her team to choose a card and read the card aloud. This student will then move ahead the number of plus spaces listed on the card or move backwards the number of minus spaces listed on the card. For example, the card, helping your teacher (+4) would enable a student to move ahead four spaces. The card, hitting your friend (-5) would enable a student to move backwards five spaces. If the student has just started the game and is on the first space when a minus card is drawn, the student does not move. Play continues until one student finishes the line for his/her team. This team is awarded 10 points. Both students sit down with their team and two new students are chosen for the game. Play continues until you call time. The winner is the team who has acquired the most points.

FOLLOW-UP

Focus discussion on the positive ways that good manners can get you ahead. Also discuss ways in which negative manners prevent you from getting ahead. Ask the students to brainstorm positive manners. Ask the students to share several ways manners can get you ahead or prevent you from getting ahead.

MANNERS CARDS

Manners Cards

YOU HELPED THE TEACHER.

+4

Manners Cards

YOU GAVE YOUR SEAT TO AN ELDERLY PERSON.

+6

Manners Cards

YOU BULLIED A KID IN LINE.

-6

Manners Cards

YOU SAID "YES MA'AM."

+3

Manners Cards

YOU HIT A FRIEND.

-5

Manners Cards

YOU BROKE YOUR NEIGHBOR'S WINDOW ON PURPOSE.

-6

© 1997 by YouthLight, Inc.

Manners Cards

YOU WERE A GOOD SPORT WHEN YOUR TEAM LOST THE SOCCER GAME.

+5

Manners Cards

YOU PICKED UP LITTER.

+4

Manners Cards

YOU HELPED A FRIEND PICK UP BOOKS.

+3

Manners Cards

YOU COVERED YOUR MOUTH WHEN YOU COUGHED.

+2

Manners Cards

YOU ASKED TO BORROW A PENCIL, INSTEAD OF TAKING ONE.

+3

Manners Cards

YOU WERE HONEST TO YOUR TEACHER.

+4

Manners Cards

You SAID YOU
WERE SORRY
WHEN YOU DID
SOMETHING
WRONG.

+4

Manners Cards

You DID NOT
INTERRUPT YOUR
TEACHER WHEN SHE
WAS TALKING.

+3

Manners Cards

You PULLED YOUR
FRIEND'S HAIR.

-3

Manners Cards

You STOLE
A PENCIL.

-3

Manners Cards

You SAID,
"EXCUSE ME"
WHEN YOU BUMPED
INTO SOMEONE.

+4

Manners Cards

You TURNED OVER
A CHAIR TO DRAW
ATTENTION TO
YOURSELF.

-5

POWER PLAY

Manners Cards

YOU GOOFED OFF
IN CLASS.

-5

Manners Cards

YOU WERE QUIET
DURING THE TEST.

+5

Manners Cards

YOU SAID,
"PLEASE."

+3

Manners Cards

YOU SNEAKED UP
ON YOUR TEACHER
AND TRIED TO
SCARE HIM/HER.

-2

Manners Cards

YOU ROLLED YOUR
EYES AT YOUR
TEACHER.

-6

Manners Cards

YOU WORE CLEAN
CLOTHES AT
SCHOOL.

+6

YOU WERE CAREFUL NOT TO TEAR UP YOUR FRIEND'S AIRPLANE.

+4

YOU CLEANED UP WHEN ASKED TO DO SO.

+4

YOU SPIT ON YOUR FRIEND.

-6

YOU RAN DOWN THE HALLS.

-3

YOU STEPPED ON A CAT ON PURPOSE.

-8

YOU PAYED ATTENTION IN CLASS.

+5

Manners Cards

YOU SLAPPED
YOUR FRIEND.

-8

Manners Cards

YOU SHARED
WITH A FRIEND.

+6

Manners Cards

YOU SAID
A CUSS WORD.

-6

Manners Cards

YOU SHRUGGED
YOUR SHOULDERS
AT THE TEACHER.

-4

Manners Cards

YOU OPENED THE
DOOR FOR
SOMEONE TO
GO IN FIRST.

+5

Manners Cards

YOU ATE
WITH YOUR
MOUTH SHUT.

+4

SOAP IT[1]

Grade Levels: 3-Middle School
Time: 30 Minutes

PURPOSE
To help students distinguish between appropriate and inappropriate words or phrases and help them to choose other words during difficult situations.

MATERIALS NEEDED
Appropriate and Inappropriate response cards.

OBJECT
To win points for your team by calling out "Soap It" first.

Procedures

1. Define inappropriate words and phrases as rude, crude, and lewd. Explain that many television shows, movies, and people are using words and phrases that are not appropriate for use at school. Ask the students to use a good model to determine appropriate use of words by asking themselves whether their teacher or principal would say the word or phrase. If they would not use the word or phrase, then it is inappropriate to use and students are instructed to call, "Soap it."

2. Divide the group into two teams.

3. The leader calls out different statements which require two opposing team members to call out "Soap It" if the statement describes an inappropriate phrase. The two members are determined before each round of play.

4. The first team member calling out "Soap It" for an inappropriate phrase (indicated with a blank, blank" statement) wins a point for their team.

5. The team loses a point if an appropriate phrase is used by the lead and "Soap It" is called out by mistake or if an inappropriate response is not caught.

SOAP IT APPROPRIATE RESPONSE CARDS

Soap It Appropriate Response Cards	Soap It Appropriate Response Cards	Soap It Appropriate Response Cards
Someone calls another person a name that person says, "Don't be rude."	**A carpenter hits his finger by accident with a hammer. He says "Oh bazooka!"**	**A friend makes a failing grade and says, "Oh, my golly!"**
Soap It Appropriate Response Cards	Soap It Appropriate Response Cards	Soap It Appropriate Response Cards
A criminal in a movie is caught by the police and says, "Crud!"	**A TV sitcom comedienne makes fun of another character's mistake and the character say, "For Pete's sake!"**	**One bully keeps scaring another student and that student says "I'm not afraid of you."**
Soap It Appropriate Response Cards	Soap It Appropriate Response Cards	Soap It Appropriate Response Cards
A cartoon character says, "Oh, raspberries!"	**You lose your homework and say, "Drat it!"**	**You trip and fall down in front of others and say, "Phooey!"**

SOAP IT INAPPROPRIATE RESPONSE CARDS

Soap It Inappropriate Response Cards	Soap It Inappropriate Response Cards	Soap It Inappropriate Response Cards
Someone drops their pencil and says, "_____, _____!"	**Someone calls another person a name and that person says, "_____, _____!"**	**A carpenter hits his finger by accident with a hammer. He says, "_____, _____!"**

Soap It Inappropriate Response Cards	Soap It Inappropriate Response Cards	Soap It Inappropriate Response Cards
One bully keeps scaring another student and that student says "_____, _____!"	A cartoon character says, "_____, _____!"	You lose your homework and say, "_____, _____!"
A criminal in a movie is caught by the police and says, "_____, _____!"	A TV sitcom comedienne makes fun of another character's mistake and that character says, "_____, _____!"	A friend makes a failing grade and says, "_____, _____!"

FOLLOW-UP

Ask the students the following questions:

- Why are some words and phrases inappropriate?

- How can this be compared to using good manners?

- How do you feel when you see or hear inappropriate words?

- What happens when students consistently use inappropriate words?

- How would the use of inappropriate words affect you in the following activities?

  a. Getting a job
  b. Talking to the principal
  c. Talking to a friend's parents
  d. Talking to a store manager about a return
  e. Trying to get a girl/boy friend
  f. Hanging out with the "gang"

Ask students to brainstorm a list of negative and positive results of using inappropriate words or phrases and compare the lists.

ATTITUDE TUNE UP

Grade Levels: K-5

Time: 30 Minutes

PURPOSE

To encourage changes in behavior and thinking when necessary.

MATERIALS NEEDED

Attitude Tune Up Station Cards
(reproduced & cutout)
Scorecard (index cards or notebook paper)

OBJECT

To make it through the road course with as many points as possible.

PROCEDURES

1. Divide students into small five teams of four to five students.

2. Make a road course around desks around the room. Keep it simple and mark four stations or stopping points with numbers such as 1-Asking Station, 2-Answering Station, 3-Actions Station, and 4-Attention Station. At each station, give the team a set of situation cards depicting a particular attitude related to that station (for example, for stations #1 and #2, appropriate body language and tone used in asking or answering questions, for station #3, the acceptable actions to demonstrate when following directions, and for station #4, the best way to pay attention). See Procedure #5 for more examples.

3. Ask one of the small groups to act as qualifying judges at each station while one team at a time goes through the road course. When the participating team finishes the road course, they

take the place of the team at station #1 and the former judges at station #4 go on the road course while judges at station #1 go to station #2; 2 goes to station #3; 3 goes to station #4. Continue rotating until all teams have finished the road course.

4. Place Station Cards with situations that depict one of the Attitude Tune Up A's (asking, answering, actions, and attention) at each station. The qualifying station team reads the Station Cards to the participating team. Any member on the participating team is selected by one of the qualifying judges to answer any one of the cards. The card may be repeated as many times as necessary by the judge(s). If the team answers correctly, they get five points, if the team answers the card incorrectly, the team gets zero points.

5. In addition, the participating team must answer with an appropriate attitude in order to be awarded five points by the judge(s). If the team answers with an inappropriate attitude, zero points are earned. One judge reads the cards while the other judges watch the team's attitude and attention. For example, the Asking Station judges listen for good manners with use of words such as "please" and "may I." The Answering Station will listen for good answering words such as "yes ma'am," "no ma'am," "yes sir," "no sir," "thank you," and a friendly tone. The Action Station watches for attention being paid to the speaker, hands and feet still, and hands up when answering a question. The Attention Station judge(s) could ask one or two questions about what they've read.

6. Play continues until all teams have gone through the check points.

FOLLOW-UP

Ask the students the following questions:

- Which Attitude Station was the easiest or most difficult for you to demonstrate?

- Why do we need to work on tuning up our attitudes?

- What can happen if we don't get an attitude tune up?

ATTITUDE TUNE UP STATION CARDS

Asking

Asking **ASK ME FOR A PENCIL.**	*Asking* **ASK FOR MORE TIME TO WORK ON A PROJECT.**
Asking **ASK ME FOR THE SALT.**	*Asking* **ASK FOR ANOTHER PIECE OF CAKE.**
Asking **ASK FOR SOME HELP FROM THE TEACHER.**	*Asking* **ASK FOR A TURN ON THE SWING.**

Answering

(Needs more than yes or no)

Answering

ARE YOU GOING TO

_____

ELEMENTARY/MIDDLE
SCHOOL?

Answering

HAVE YOU CLEANED
YOUR ROOM?

Answering

DID YOU DO YOUR
HOMEWORK?

Answering

WILL YOU PICK
UP THAT PAPER?

Answering

DO YOU NEED SOME
MONEY FOR LUNCH?

Answering

HERE IS SOME
CANDY.

Attention

Attention

I'm going to give you directions for the Attitude Adjustment Road Course. First of all, pay attention, and watch how you ask questions. Use "please" and "may I…"when you ask questions. Watch how you answer people . Use "yes, ma'am" and "no, ma'am" or "yes, sir"and "no, sir." Your actions should be friendly. Do you have any questions?

Attention

You need to listen to all of the directions. Stop at each station and receive points if you pass the test at the station. Do you have any questions?

Attention

Directions are important for everyone to listen to. Your team will go to each station and demonstrate good attention, good actions, good asking and answering skills. Be sure to be on your best behavior to earn five points for good attitude.

Attention

We hope all of you have good attitudes. Good attitudes are like good manners. We will give you five points if you show us good attention skills. You will get zero points for poor attention skills. Make sure your eyes are on the speaker and your feet and hands are still.

Actions: (items needed - a book, a chair)

Actions

GIVE ME THE BOOK, PLEASE.

Actions

RAISE YOUR HAND, PLEASE.

Actions

LET'S SHAKE HANDS.

Actions

FACE THE BACK OF THE ROOM, PLEASE.

Actions

SIT DOWN, PLEASE.

Actions

HOP ON ONE FOOT, PLEASE.

Actions

STAND UP, PLEASE.

Actions

FACE THE FRONT OF THE ROOM, PLEASE.

WHAT IF?

Grade Levels: K-5

Time: 30 Minutes

PURPOSES

To motivate students to think proactively. To encourage students to think ahead about the possible consequences of their actions.

MATERIALS NEEDED

What If Point Cards (reproduced & cutout)
2 Bean bags or other throwing objects

OBJECT

To accumulate more points than the other team by throwing the bean bag onto point cards and answering questions correctly.

Procedures

1. Divide the class into two teams and give each team one bean bag.

2. Place the What If Point Cards randomly in the middle of the floor face down.

3. Ask one student to throw his/her team's bag so that it lands on or near one point card. Award the team this number of points if they answer the question appropriately. The team has three chances to either throw the bag directly on a point card or throw the bag so that it touches the point card. If the bag does not touch a card in three throws, play goes to the other team

4. After the first team answers the question, award them the points listed for a correct response, or no points for an incorrect response. Then the other team takes a turn. The game continues as time allows. Play can continue until each group has a certain number of points or until time runs out.

FOLLOW-UP

Discuss the following with your students:

- The importance of being able to deal with situations quickly.

- Whether or not you should always be honest in every situation.

- Thinking through consequences before determining an action.

WHAT IF CARDS

What If Cards

25

WHAT WOULD YOU DO IF YOUR FRIEND CALLED
YOU A NERD?

What If Cards

100

WHAT WOULD YOU DO IF YOUR FRIEND MADE
FUN OF YOUR SHOES?

What If Cards

50

WHAT WOULD YOU DO IF YOUR FRIEND CALLED
YOU A DUMMY?

What If Cards

25

WHAT WOULD YOU DO IF YOUR FRIEND MADE
FUN OF YOUR DAD?

What If Cards

75

WHAT WOULD YOU DO IF YOUR
FRIEND MADE FUN OF YOUR MOM?

What If Cards

50

WHAT WOULD YOU DO IF YOUR FRIEND
MADE FUN OF YOUR HAIR?

What If Cards

75

WHAT WOULD YOU DO IF YOUR
FRIEND WOULD NOT COME TO
YOUR BIRTHDAY PARTY?

What If Cards

50

WHAT IF SOMEONE SAID YOU
WERE TOO SHORT?

POWER PLAY

What If Cards

100

WHAT WOULD YOU DO IF YOU WEREN'T INVITED TO A BIRTHDAY PARTY?

What If Cards

75

WHAT WOULD YOU DO IF SOMEONE DIDN'T LIKE YOUR RACE?

What If Cards

25

WHAT WOULD YOU DO IF SOMEONE SAID YOU WERE TOO FAT?

What If Cards

100

WHAT WOULD YOU DO IF SOMEONE DIDN'T LIKE YOUR NEIGHBORHOOD?

What If Cards

25

WHAT WOULD YOU DO IF YOUR FRIEND CALLED YOUR MOTHER A FAT SLOB?

What If Cards

100

WHAT WOULD YOU DO IF YOUR FRIEND SAID NOBODY LIKED YOU?

What If Cards

50

WHAT WOULD YOU DO IF YOUR FRIEND CALLED YOU AN IDIOT?

What If Cards

125

WHAT WOULD YOU DO IF PEOPLE SAID YOU WERE UGLY?

What If Cards

75

WHAT WOULD YOU DO IF YOUR FRIEND CALLED YOU STUPID?

What If Cards

150

WHAT WOULD YOU DO IF PEOPLE SAID YOU WERE A NOBODY?

What If Cards

25

WHAT WOULD YOU DO IF YOUR FRIENDS SAID YOU WEREN'T COOL BECAUSE YOU DIDN'T SMOKE?

What If Cards

150

WHAT WOULD YOU DO IF SOMEONE SAID YOU WEREN'T COOL BECAUSE YOU DIDN'T DRINK A BEER?

What If Cards

50

WHAT WOULD YOU DO IF YOUR FRIENDS SAID YOU WEREN'T COOL BECAUSE YOU DIDN'T TAKE DRUGS?

What If Cards

200

WHAT WOULD YOU DO IF YOUR FRIENDS WERE STEALING FROM A STORE AND YOU WERE WITH THEM?

What If Cards

75

WHAT WOULD YOU DO IF YOUR FRIENDS SAID YOU WERE GOING TO FAIL YOUR GRADE?

What If Cards

100

WHAT WOULD YOU DO IF YOU KNEW YOUR FRIEND WAS BEING ABUSED?

TAKE FIVE

Grade Levels: 2-5

Time: 30 Minutes

PURPOSES

To teach students appropriate social responses to situations they might encounter and to think fast in these situations.

MATERIALS NEEDED

Grid block diagram drawn on chalkboard
Statements for Take Five
Basket
2 team markers
Small papers numbered from 1-25

OBJECTS

To be the first team to get five blocks in a row either vertically, horizontally, or diagonally and to obtain the most points answering questions.

PROCEDURES

1. Divide the group into small groups of four or five.

2. Draw a large grid on the chalk board or a large sheet of paper. As shown on the next page, the grid has five blocks across, and five down. Number the blocks from one to twenty-five. Also, write the numbers one through twenty-five on small slips of paper and place them in a basket or box. Place a star on some of the slips of paper indicating an instant winner for the group. Award this group a small prize.

3. Ask each team to draw a number from the basket, then ask the team to respond to the statement corresponding to that number. This team has to "take five" seconds to respond to each statement. If the team is able to respond to the statement within five seconds, the

team gets 10 points and is able to place their team marker on that number of the game board. (This could be a symbol on the chalk board or any other marker you would like to use.) If the team comes up with an additional response to the statement, they may be awarded five bonus points for every correct response over the number asked for on the statement. For example, if a statement asked for three responses and they gave four, they would be awarded 15 points--10 for the correct response to the question and 5 for the bonus response.

4. Play continues as time allows. Points are totalled and winners declared. Winners may also be declared if a team has their marker in five consecutive boxes either vertically, horizontally, or diagonally.

TAKE FIVE BOARD

1	2	3	4	5
6	7	8	9	10
11	12	13	14	15
16	17	18	19	20
21	22	23	24	25

FOLLOW-UP

Tell the group that often they only have five seconds to make very important decisions. Emphasize the importance of thinking quickly on your feet.

- Name some real situations when you have to think quickly.
- Was it difficult to think quickly? Do you think you can make incorrect decisions when you think so quickly?
- What would help you to make a really fast decision with your friends?

Statements for Take Five

1. Name two ways of making friends.
2. Name two things to do if you get lost in a store.
3. Name three fun things to do without taking drugs.
4. Name two ways to succeed in school.
5. Name three good character traits.
6. Name four things to be when you grow up.
7. Name two things which are unhealthy for you to do.
8. Name three things which will get you suspended.
9. Name two things to do to avoid a fight.
10. Name two consequences to fighting.
11. Name two feelings that could lead to fighting.
12. Name one thing to do when people talk about you.
13. Name two responses you can give to adults when you don't agree with them.
14. Name two things you can say to yourself that will cool you down and hopefully stop a fight.
15. Name two ways to be responsible in school.
16. Name two ways to be responsible at home.
17. Name three ways to help people.
18. Name two things to say instead of cursing.
19. Name one thing to say if your friend is stealing and you know it.
20. Name two things to do if someone is touching you inappropriately.
21. Name two things that cause fights.
22. Name two things to say to yourself when you've made a mistake.
23. Name two things to do when you feel frustrated.
24. Name two ways to help yourself pay attention.
25. Name two ways to keep your desk organized.
26. Name two ways to calm yourself when feeling frustrated.
27. Name two ways to get yourself to complete a task.
28. Name two things to remember when doing your work in class.
29. Name two things important to staying on task in the classroom.
30. Name three things to tell yourself when you've done a good job.
31. Name one thing to do if one friend won't play with you anymore.
32. Name two reasons kids might want to take drugs.

   * Note: The board can be made larger or smaller to accommodate the necessary numbering of questions.

Section IV:

COOPERATION

Educational curriculum requires that students have the ability to work with others in different groupings. In order for this teaching technique to be successful, students need to practice skills to enhance the success of their cooperative endeavors. Students need to know that cooperation involves taking turns, sharing, helping others, doing unpleasant assignments, planning with others, participating, and keeping the group effort and achievement of the utmost importance. These skills demand that the self is replaced by a collective "we."

The following activities encourage cooperation and learning of cooperative skills through fun activities. Students are encouraged to produce results, follow instructions, and work together to accomplish group goals. The activities are fun and different, yet accomplish the very important goal of teaching children the art of cooperation.

Wahwahlanawah

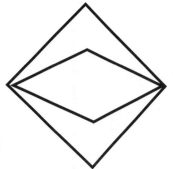

Grade Levels: 4-Middle School

Time: 30 Minutes

Purpose

To help students with problem-solving, cooperating, and planning skills.

Materials Needed

Paper
Tape
Timer

Object

To make as many Wahwahlanawahs as possible and compete against your team's previous count.

Procedures

1. Divide students into small teams.

2. Challenge students to make as many functional Wahwahlanawahs as they can in a certain amount of time.

3. Directions for making Wahwahlanawahs:
   1. Fold an 81/2" x 11" paper in half lengthwise.
      Fold each half down on the outside to the first fold, also lengthwise like making a paper airplane. The paper should now have three lengthwise folds, and be very thin and long.
   2. Fold each corner down in opposite directions in a triangle shape and tape.
   3. Crease exactly in half in the middle lining up the two triangle shapes. It should look like a boat.
   4. Open at the longer side to make a duck "quacker" beak shape that moves up and down.

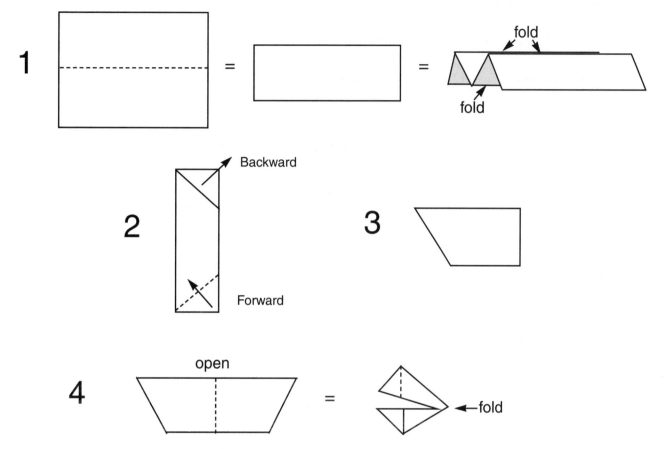

4. Each team must educate the members on how to make the Wahwahlanawahs, organize the jobs needed, and organize the materials. (For example: assembly line, individual work, etc.) Teams are given 5-10 minutes to practice.

5. Give the teams three minutes to work.

6. After time is called, one member from each team must check and count the workable products made by the other team. Give one point to each team for each workable Wahwahlanawah.

7. Repeat the activity several times to see if each team can exceed their first number of Wahwahlanawahs. There is only competition within the team to better their score.

FOLLOW-UP

Discuss the following with your students:

- How did you organize your team?

- What helped you the most on your team?

- What didn't help you on your team?

- What did you learn to do differently each time?

WORDLES™

M LOVE E

ME QUIT ME HEAD NT HEELS

Grade Levels: 3-Middle School   **Time: 30 Minutes**

PURPOSE
To Practice cooperation and participation.

MATERIALS NEEDED
WORDLES™ on index cards

OBJECT
To work together to solve word puzzles.

PROCEDURES

1. Define a **WORDLE**™ as a type of word puzzle that makes a phrase or message when letters, words, or spaces are arranged in a meaningful pattern.

    Examples:

    Side By Side = | SIDE SIDE | Apartment= | ME NT |

    | issue, issue, issue, issue, issue, issue, issue, issue, issue, issue | = **Tennis Shoe**

    | ME QUIT | = **Quit Following Me**

2. Divide the students into small teams of four or five.

3. Give a different set of four index cards containing Wordles™ to each group.

4. Ask each team to work together to solve the WORDLES™.

5. Ask each team to have answers written down by a team secretary and to hand them in to the leader to be checked.

6. When the team finishes a set of WORDLES™ with 100% accuracy, give the team a small treat.

7. Next, give another set of cards to the team. Ask the team to try to solve as many sets as they can, earning small treats each time. As the card sets are turned in, rotate them to another team.

FOLLOW-UP

Discuss the following with your students:

- How did your team work together?

- How well did everyone participate?

- What would have helped your team solve more puzzles?

WORDLES™ taken from <u>Silver Bullets.</u> by Karl Rohnke, Kendall/Hunt Publishing Co., 1984, p.102-105.

BALLOON BOP

Grade Levels: K-5

Time: 15 Minutes

PURPOSES

To demonstrate the value of cooperation in the classroom. To help students develop self-control, listening & problem-solving skills.

MATERIALS NEEDED

One balloon

OBJECT

To work as a team and keep the balloon from touching the ground while staying seated.

PROCEDURES

1. Ask students to sit on the floor (preferably with their legs crossed in front).

2. Explain the rules of the game:

    - Students must remain seated.
    - Students cannot get up off their knees to hit the balloon.
    - Students cannot crawl to get the balloon.
    - If the balloon goes out of bounds or beyond the child's reach, the game is called.
    - Students are challenged to keep the balloon in the air by batting it 100 times.
    - Students are told that either everyone will win or everyone will lose.

3. Stop the game each time the ballon goes out of bounds or a student gets off his/her knees. Encourage the discussion found on page 204.

- What is the problem?
- How can we solve the problem?
- Let's implement the solution.

4. Play continues until the team is successful.

FOLLOW-UP

Discuss the following with your students when they achieve their goal:

- How did we accomplish our goal (cooperation, listening, following directions, working together)?
- When we had problems, what did we do?
- Did everyone do their part by listening carefully and cooperating?

Discuss the following with your students if they did not achieve their goal:

- What happened so that we did not accomplish our goal?
- What did we do right?
- What could we do differently next time?

Section V:

Character building involves exposing children to the virtues agreed upon by citizens as necessary for a democratic society to thrive. Without honesty, helpfulness to others, happiness, gentleness, kindness, responsibility, trustworthiness, patience, and many other positive characteristics, a very negative environment would exist. Character building is an important part of a society's basic functioning and existence.

The activities that follow emphasize positive character traits and encourage children to adopt these traits themselves. Students are encouraged to make wise choices while developing behaviors to not only to make the world a better place, but also to help themselves be better able to reach their own personal goals.

CHARACTER BUILDING

"MIRROR, MIRROR ON THE WALL"

Grade Levels: 3-5

Time: 30 Minutes

PURPOSE
To discover the character qualities in a person that are most important.

MATERIALS NEEDED
Role Play Cards (reproduced & cutout)
Adapted review of Snow White

OBJECT
To be the first to identify a character trait
that is being role-played.

PROCEDURES

1. Divide the group into small teams of 5-6 students.

2. Ask one person or several on a team to choose a card to role-play.

3. Instruct the group that during each person's turn, they are to repeat the phrase from Snow White;

    "Mirror, Mirror on the wall, who is the fairest of them all?"

4. Ask the rest of the groups to take turns deciding if the role-play exemplifies the fairest or nicest type of character, or the worst type of character. The team that answers first earns one point.To earn five extra points, the team must identify the character quality. For example, if the characteristic being role-played is correctly identified as fairest or nicest type of character, the answering team receives one point. If the answering team can also name the character quality, such as kindness, that team gets five extra points.

VARIATION

Role-play can be with or without dialogue. If there is dialogue in the role-plays, caution the players not to state the character quality.

FOLLOW-UP

Discuss the following with your students:

- Which quality was the most difficult for you to identify?

- How did you feel while you were acting out the fairest qualities of a person's character?

- How did you feel while you were acting out the ugliest qualities?

- Why are the fairest qualities important?

- Which fairest qualities do you have or do you see in others?

- Which fairest qualities are you going to try to work on? How?

The Adapted Review of
Snow White

Once upon a time, as you remember, a beautiful, kind young princess named Snow White lived in a castle with her wicked step mother, the Queen. The Queen was very jealous of Snow White's beauty and goodness, and would always check her magic mirror on the wall to ask who was the fairest in the land.

The Queen would say, "Mirror, Mirror on the wall. Who is the fairest of them all?" The Queen always wanted to be the prettiest and would rage if her mirror named anyone else as the prettiest. She found it particularly unbearable to hear the mirror reply,

"Snow White is the fairest of them all."

Eventually, Snow White's good positive qualities of character won out over the negative terrible qualities of the Queen; Snow White was saved by a Prince who admired her while the Queen was destroyed.

ROLE-PLAY CARDS FOR MIRROR, MIRROR ON THE WALL

Role-Play Cards for Mirror, Mirror on the Wall

Someone who shares things

Role-Play Cards for Mirror, Mirror on the Wall

Someone who is rough

Role-Play Cards for Mirror, Mirror on the Wall

Someone who is gentle

Role-Play Cards for Mirror, Mirror on the Wall

Someone who is thoughtful

Role-Play Cards for Mirror, Mirror on the Wall

Someone who is caring

Role-Play Cards for Mirror, Mirror on the Wall

Someone who is thoughtless

Role-Play Cards for
Mirror, Mirror on the Wall

Someone who
is kind

Role-Play Cards for
Mirror, Mirror on the Wall

Someone who is happy

Role-Play Cards for
Mirror, Mirror on the Wall

Someone who is selfish

Role-Play Cards for
Mirror, Mirror on the Wall

Someone who is peaceful

Role-Play Cards for
Mirror, Mirror on the Wall

Someone who is unhappy

Role-Play Cards for
Mirror, Mirror on the Wall

Someone who hits others

Role-Play Cards for
Mirror, Mirror on the Wall

Someone who is fussy

Role-Play Cards for
Mirror, Mirror on the Wall

Someone who is
helpful to others

Role-Play Cards for
Mirror, Mirror on the Wall

*Someone who
studies hard*

Role-Play Cards for
Mirror, Mirror on the Wall

*Someone who
is always sad*

Role-Play Cards for
Mirror, Mirror on the Wall

*Someone who
doesn't care*

Role-Play Cards for
Mirror, Mirror on the Wall

*Someone who
is bossy*

Role-Play Cards for
Mirror, Mirror on the Wall

Someone who argues

Role-Play Cards for
Mirror, Mirror on the Wall

*Someone who
is jealous*

Role-Play Cards for
Mirror, Mirror on the Wall

Someone who gossips

Role-Play Cards for
Mirror, Mirror on the Wall

*Someone who
calls names*

DRESS UP, DRESS DOWN

Grade Levels: 2-5

Time: 30 Minutes

PURPOSE

To help students recognize consequences of behavior choices.

MATERIALS NEEDED

Dress up clothes (wigs, socks, shirts, etc.)
Dress Up, Dress Down Character Cards
(reproduced & cutout)

OBJECT

To draw Character Cards and collect as
many rewards as possible by drawing
good character cards.

PROCEDURES

1. Discuss positive and negative character or reputation-building characteristics. Solicit examples of good and poor characteristics from the class.

2. Let the class nominate a volunteer demonstrator. Ask the volunteer to choose a class member who will select a Dress Up, Dress Down Character Card. Character Cards list either good or poor character building actions.

3. If the chosen character card depicts a poor characteristic, the volunteer must put on a funny looking Dress Up item. Some examples are a wig, a hat, cape, glasses with a nose, etc. Draw a comparison between how looking silly can be like having a bad reputation.

4. If the chosen character card depicts a good characteristic, the student who drew that card receives a reward, perhaps a sticker, a hand stamp, a candy treat, etc. Imply that looking good or feeling good can be compared to a good reputation.

5. Ask students to take turns drawing a card and responding as to whether the trait listed on the card is a good or poor characteristic.

6. In the end, the volunteer will look rather silly. Discuss how poor characteristics may get us attention, but may end up making us look silly in front of our friends. Bad behavior choices may also gain us a bad reputation of being uncool or a person that no one wants to hang out with.

VARIATION

Place the behavior cards in an envelope. Let the class nominate a volunteer to be the "dress up" person. Choose other students to pick a card. Have a race to see if three positive trait cards can be chosen before three negative trait cards. If a positive trait card is chosen, the volunteer keeps the card. If a negative card is chosen, the person who draws the card chooses something from the dress up bag for the volunteer to put on. Ideally, the items are in a dark plastic bag so the students cannot see what is being chosen. If three positive cards are chosen before three negative cards, declare the person dressing up (the volunteer) a winner and give them a small prize. This, of course, symbolizes how one is truly a winner when choosing good character traits. Then choose a new volunteer. Rename this "Trick-or-Treat" during Halloween time.

FOLLOW-UP

Discuss the following with your students:
- What have you learned about poor behavior choices or bad reputations?
- Are good behavior choices easy or difficult?
- What situations make it most difficult for a person to choose good behavior?
- Is it important to work on having a good reputation? Why?
- What do you actually win when choosing positive character traits?
- What do you actually lose when choosing negative character traits?

DRESS UP, DRESS DOWN CHARACTER CARDS

(For the game, mix Negative and Positive Character Cards together).

NEGATIVE CHARACTERISTICS

Dress Up, Dress Down
Negative Character Cards

This person gets angry and throwards books.

Dress Up, Dress Down
Negative Character Cards

This person calls the other students names.

Dress Up, Dress Down
Negative Character Cards

This person yells at the teacher.

Dress Up, Dress Down
Negative Character Cards

This person doesn't do homework.

Dress Up, Dress Down
Negative Character Cards

When there is a test, this person cheats.

Dress Up, Dress Down
Negative Character Cards

This person will not pay attention or listen in class.

POWER PLAY

© 1997 by YouthLight, Inc.

Dress Up, Dress Down
Negative Character Cards

This person always says
untrue things about others.

Dress Up, Dress Down
Negative Character Cards

This person steals
money from others.

Dress Up, Dress Down
Negative Character Cards
This person just plays with
one group and talks
badly about others.

Dress Up, Dress Down
Negative Character Cards

This person shoves
and pushes in line.

Dress Up, Dress Down
Negative Character Cards
This person wants his/her
way with everything and
will not cooperate.

Dress Up, Dress Down
Negative Character Cards

This person acts like a bully
and wants to fight others.

Dress Up, Dress Down
Negative Character Cards

This person gossips
about others.

Dress Up, Dress Down
Negative Character Cards

This person takes
other people's pencils.

POSITIVE CHARACTERISTICS

Dress Up, Dress Down
Positive Character Cards

This person tries to do his/her best on his/her school work.

Dress Up, Dress Down
Positive Character Cards

This person respects the property of others.

Dress Up, Dress Down
Positive Character Cards

This person always says "Yes Ma'am" and "Yes Sir."

Dress Up, Dress Down
Positive Character Cards

This person tells the truth even when it might get him/her in trouble.

Dress Up, Dress Down
Positive Character Cards

This person pays attention in class.

Dress Up, Dress Down
Positive Character Cards

This person follows directions.

Dress Up, Dress Down
Positive Character Cards

This person does not touch things that do not belong to him/her.

Dress Up, Dress Down
Positive Character Cards

This person is friendly to others.

Dress Up, Dress Down
Positive Character Cards
This person tries to have
homework turned
in on time.

Dress Up, Dress Down
Positive Character Cards
This person includes
others.

Dress Up, Dress Down
Positive Character Cards
This person is kind
to elderly people.

Dress Up, Dress Down
Positive Character Cards
This person is polite
and well mannered.

Dress Up, Dress Down
Positive Character Cards
This person doesn't
interrupt others.

Dress Up, Dress Down
Positive Character Cards
This person
follows directions.

Dress Up, Dress Down
Positive Character Cards
This person does not
touch things that do not
belong to him/her.

Dress Up, Dress Down
Positive Character Cards
This person is friendly
to others.

CHARACTER PARADE

Grade Levels: 2-5

Time: 30 Minutes

PURPOSE
To help students recognize positive character qualities.

MATERIALS NEEDED
Character Cards (reproduced & cutout)
Numbers
Hats

OBJECT
To draw a positive character card and participate in the Character Parade.

PROCEDURES

1. Define character as a person's pattern of behaving or their personality traits; being honest is a positive character quality and being dishonest is a negative character quality.

2. Give each student a different number. That number is put into a hat to be drawn out.

3. Draw a number from the hat and ask that student to take a Character Card and read it aloud. Character Cards describe positive and negative character traits which name and describe a character quality. Note: discard numbers after you draw them, don't place them back in the hat.

4. Ask the rest of the group to act as judges and raise their hands to vote for that characteristic being a positive character quality or not a positive character quality.

5. If the positive votes win and you concur, the student will keep the card until parade time. If the negative votes win, the student will sit down, and serve as an audience member for the parade.

6. Present a Character Parade at the end of the game. Ask each person who had a positive characteristic to give the leader his/her card. Read the card aloud while the student parades around at the front of the room. If possible, play music and provide different hats to make it a Bonnet Parade or Easter Parade. Old hats can add spice, variety, and fun.

7. Give each student in the parade rousing applause.

FOLLOW-UP

Discuss the following with your students:

- Was it difficult recognizing a positive character quality?
- If you were in the parade, how did you feel?
- Which quality was your favorite character quality? Why?

Character Cards

Character Cards
Respectfulness

listening to others and
letting them have
their turn

Character Cards
Happiness

being content no matter what
happens

Character Cards
Responsibility

doing your job without being
told

Character Cards
Patience

not hurrying through things

Character Cards
Kindness

thinking of another
person first

Character Cards
Trustworthiness

being honest and dependable

Character Cards
Gentleness

being careful, not rough

Character Cards
Helpfulness

helping others

Character Cards
Peacefulness

being easy to get
along with, not arguing
or fighting

Character Cards
Hatefulness

being mean

Character Cards
Hard Working

concentrating and making sure
the job is done right

Character Cards
Revengefulness

trying to pay someone back for
wrongdoing that you think they
have done to you

Character Cards
Unhappiness

being dissatisfied with many
things

Character Cards
Carelessness

being rough and
not taking care

Character Cards
Impatience

wanting to hurry and get
things done without care

Character Cards
Unkindness

not being nice to others
and being disrespectful

Character Cards ## Unforgiving *always remembering the wrong someone has done to you*	**Character Cards** ## Irresponsibility *not doing what has been asked of you*
Character Cards ## Dishonesty *not telling the truth and not being able to be trusted*	**Character Cards** ## Disrespectfulness *not acknowledging others feelings*
Character Cards ## Laziness *not doing what needs to be done*	**Character Cards** ## Gratefulness *being thankful for what you have*
Character Cards ## Argumentative *fussing about many things*	**Character Cards** ## Honesty *doing what is right even when no one is watching you*

WHO AM I?

Grade Levels: 1-5

Time: 30 Minutes

PURPOSE

To help students recognize different characteristics in others' personalities.

MATERIALS NEEDED

Who Am I Cards (reproduced & cutout)
10-rung ladder drawn on poster board
A place marker

OBJECT

To get one point by guessing the personality characteristic after asking ten questions.

PROCEDURES

1. Divide students into two teams.

2. Ask one student to come forward and take a Who Am I? Character Card to determine which character role he/she will play. Tell that student to be ready to respond to the other team's questions about the characteristic from the card without showing others.

3. Instruct the other team to ask questions about the way the character would think, act, work, etc.

4. Move the team's place marker up one rung on the ladder for each question asked. At the end of 10 questions, the team must guess who the character is.

5. If they guess correctly, the team scores one point. If the team guesses incorrectly, the opposing team gets a point.

FOLLOW-UP

Discuss the following with your students:

- Which characters would you enjoy being around?
- Which characters would you not like to have as friends?
- How could you improve some of these personality characteristics?

Who Am I? Character Cards

Who Am I? Character Cards	Who Am I? Character Cards
Attention Seeker	**Foolish**
Who Am I? Character Cards	Who Am I? Character Cards
Hostile	**Wise**
Who Am I? Character Cards	Who Am I? Character Cards
Apathetic (not caring)	**Tattle Tale**
Who Am I? Character Cards	Who Am I? Character Cards
Troublemaker	**Nosey**

Who Am I? Character Cards

Bossy

Who Am I? Character Cards

Stubborn

Who Am I? Character Cards

Class Clown

Who Am I? Character Cards

Bully

Who Am I? Character Cards

Hard Worker

Who Am I? Character Cards

Immature

(Babyish)

Who Am I? Character Cards

Studious

(Likes school work)

Who Am I? Character Cards

Know-It-All

Who Am I? Character Cards

Spoiled

Who Am I? Character Cards

Happy

Who Am I? Character Cards

Depressed

(Sad)

Who Am I? Character Cards

Complainer

(Cranky)

Who Am I? Character Cards

Cry Baby

Who Am I? Character Cards

A Gossip

Who Am I? Character Cards

Smart Aleck

Who Am I? Character Cards

Good Mannered

WISE MAN, FOOLISH MAN

Grade Levels: 2-5

Time: 30 Minutes

PURPOSE
To encourage good behavior choices and decisions.

MATERIALS NEEDED
Wise Man, Foolish Man Character Cards
(reproduced & cutout)
Spinner
Leader's list

OBJECTS
To name as many wise or foolish actions
that are called for and to obtain
as many points as possible.

PROCEDURES

1. Divide students into teams or small groups of approximately 5-6 students.

2. Mix the Wise Man, Foolish Man Character Cards together and place them in a stack. Ask a student from one team to draw a card, and spin the spinner.

3. The leader has the main list of wise and foolish actions. If a Foolish Man Card is drawn, read the wise actions for the location stated on the card to the responding team. Call out the same number of items from the list as the spinner displays. Then the responding team must counter by calling out what the Foolish Man does in the location.

4. Ask the team to call out the number of characteristics displayed on the spinner. The number on the spinner will also determine the number of points to be won. For example if

the number five is spun, the team must call out five items which are the opposite of what the leader reads from the main list. If they succeed, they win five points.

5. If the answering team gives the wrong answer, the next team gets the chance to earn the points by answering.

FOLLOW-UP

Discuss the following with your students:

- What did you learn about foolish and wise behavior?
- Is it important for someone to change their foolish behavior? Why?
- What are some consequences of foolish behavior?

Wise Man, Foolish Man Character Cards

Wise Man, Foolish Man Character Cards

Foolish man on the playground

Wise Man, Foolish Man Character Cards

Wise man on the bus

Wise Man, Foolish Man Character Cards

Wise man on the playground

Wise Man, Foolish Man Character Cards

Foolish man in the library

Wise Man, Foolish Man Character Cards

Foolish man in the auditorium

Wise Man, Foolish Man Character Cards

Wise man in the library

Wise Man, Foolish Man Character Cards

Wise man in the auditorium

Wise Man, Foolish Man Character Cards

Foolish man in the cafeteria

© 1997 by YouthLight, Inc.

Wise Man, Foolish Man Character Cards

Foolish man on the bus

Wise Man, Foolish Man Character Cards

Wise man in the cafeteria

Wise Man, Foolish Man Character Cards

Foolish man in the classroom

Wise Man, Foolish Man Character Cards

Wise man in the restroom

Wise Man, Foolish Man Character Cards

Wise man in the classroom

Wise Man, Foolish Man Character Cards

Wise man in the office

Wise Man, Foolish Man Character Cards

Foolish man in the hall

Wise Man, Foolish Man Character Cards

Foolish man in the office

POWER ☀ PLAY

Wise Man, Foolish Man Character Cards

Wise man in the hall

Wise Man, Foolish Man Character Cards

Wise man in
the special class

Wise Man, Foolish Man Character Cards

Foolish man
in the restroom

Wise Man, Foolish Man Character Cards

Foolish man in
the special class

© 1997 by YouthLight, Inc.

WISE MAN, FOOLISH MAN LEADER'S LIST

Foolish Man in the Hall

Runs
Yells
Jumps
Stands out of line
Whistles
Pushes

Wise Man in the Hall

Walks
Whispers
Tip toes
Stays in line
Walks patiently in the line
Keeps his hands to himself

Foolish Man in Class

Hums out loud
Daydreams
Laughs out loud and disturbs others
Taps his pencil
Plays with a toy
Laughs at a friend who makes a mistake
Uses a loud voice
Draws pictures instead of working
Constantly sharpens his pencils
Borrows and doesn't return pencils
Laughs when someone misbehaves
Says, "Give me my turn now."

Wise Man in the Class

Is silent
Focuses
Works
Sits quietly
Writes his school work
Ignores the person who misbehaves
Speaks with a soft voice
Reads quietly when finished with work
Gets classwork done
Returns borrowed things
Says, "May I please?"
Says, "Thank you."

Foolish Man in the Cafeteria

Runs
Pushes in the lunch line
Chews with his mouth open
Drops food on the floor
Blows food on someone
Plays with his food
Spits at people
Spits food out
Talks Loudly
Complains about food

Wise Man in the Cafeteria

Walks carefully
Waits patiently
Chews with mouth closed
Keeps food on plate
Chews food carefully & swallows
Talks softly
Says thank you for the food
Uses utensils properly
Uses napkins
Eats slowly

Foolish Man at P.E.

Hits others

Doesn't listen to the teacher's whistle

Runs in front of the moving swings

Pushes people off of the slide

Trips people in soccer

Throws the bat

Argues to be first

Fusses when a teammate doesn't do well

Doesn't play by the rules

Wise Man at P.E.

Kicks the ball only

Is careful

Listens for the teacher's whistle

Stays away from the moving swings

Sits still in the swing

Takes turns

Lays the bat down carefully

Encourages teammates who lose a game

Plays by the Rules

Foolish Man in the Auditorium

Doesn't listen to the program

Throws things

Boos at things he doesn't like

Hits others

Sits on his feet so others can't see

Talks during the performance

Laughs at everything even when it's not funny

Fidgets

Wise Man in the Auditorium

Listens to the program

Stays quiet

Keeps his hands to himself

Keeps his feet on the floor

Stays quiet

Laughs appropriately

Keeps his chair flat

Stays in his seat

Foolish Man on the Bus

Stands up

Opens windows without permission

Shouts at others

Hits others

Won't sit with others nicely

Makes faces at others

Argues with the bus driver

Eats food on the bus

Calls others names

Wise Man on the Bus

Sits down

Leaves windows alone

Whispers

Keeps his hands to himself

Listens to the bus driver

Doesn't eat food on the bus

Doesn't call others names

Ignores people who bother him

Sits with people who don't get into trouble

POWER PLAY

Foolish Man in the Library

Runs

Pushes books on the floor

Keeps books out too long

Pushes in line

Puts books back on the shelf incorrectly

Looks at pictures only and doesn't read

Tears the books

Writes in the books

Shouts

Wise Man in the Library

Walks

Keeps books on the shelf

Turns books in on time

Stands quietly in line

Keeps books in order

Reads the books

Takes good care of the books

Doesn't write in the books

Whispers

Foolish Man in the Restroom

Throws water on the floor

Throws paper on the floor

Doesn't flush

Doesn't wash his hands

Makes noise

Swings on the door

Peeks at others

Wets on the floor

Starts fights

Wise Man in the Restroom

Keeps the floor clean

Flushes

Washes his hands

Is quiet

Shuts and Opens doors carefully

Goes in the commode

Minds his own business

Doesn't fight

Puts the seat down on commode

Foolish Man in the Office

Talks back to the principal

Jumps around

Yells

Pushes someone

Disobeys the office staff

Laughs loudly

Wise Man in the Office

Is polite

Pays attention

Sits down

Talks softly

Walks quietly

Waits patiently

Foolish Man in Special Classes

Yells at the teacher

Jumps around

Bothers others

Disrupts the class

Wise Man in Special Classes

Pays attention

Works

Raises his hand

Participates in class

POT OF GOLD

Grade Levels: 3-5

Time: 30 Minutes

PURPOSE

To help students recognize the importance of patience,
persistence, planning and participating.

MATERIALS NEEDED

Four leaf clover leaves
Needle & thread (for each group)
WORDLES®
Paper (one sheet per group)
Pencil (one for each group)

OBJECT

To work as a team to form a
four leaf clover by completing four tasks.

PROCEDURES

1. Divide the students into small teams of 4-5 students each. Give them four tasks to complete in order to earn a four leaf clover, one leaf for each task. The four tasks demonstrate the four qualities of patience, persistence, planning, and participating. Introduce these activities one at a time and allow the team to work at its own pace.

2. For patience, each team member tries to thread a needle.

3. For persistence, each team has a different set of four WORDLES® to solve. Instruct the team to write down the answer on one sheet of paper that they will turn in and have checked.

4. For planning, each team plans a creative party and writes down what kind, when, where, the reason for the party, and who is invited.

5. For participating, each team member must participate in all activities. Place a marker at the team's table if you spot a lack of participation. You may remove this marker if the group begins totally participating.

6. When a four leaf clover is formed by a team, a treat is earned; candy in a gold wrapper or something chosen from a "pot of gold."

FOLLOW-UP

Discuss the following with your students:

- How did you feel when your team earned the four leaf clover?
- What helped your team to earn the four leaf clover?
- Which task or quality was the most difficult for you or your group?

COVER IT

Grade Levels: 2-5

Time: 30 Minutes

PURPOSE

To practice problem solving by deciding what values are important to having a good life.

MATERIALS NEEDED

List (next page)
Paper (for each student)
Paper squares

OBJECT

To write down eight of the correct items needed to function in society.

PROCEDURES

1. Divide students into pairs or small teams.

2. Hand out a Student's List (to each team) which has numbered items denoting things that may or may not be important to children. The pairs or small teams will use this list to decide which numbered items are most important to them. (For a "Cover It" Items Student List, see page 240.)

3. Ask the students to fold a sheet of paper until it contains eight boxes.

   Directions: Fold an 8" x 10" sheet of paper in half length-wise. Then fold it in half top to bottom two more times. When it is opened, it will have eight boxes. Ask the students to use the "Cover It" Items Student List to make a list of the numbers of the eight items most important to them on the folded sheet of paper (place one number in each box).

4. Call out the numbers of the items necessary to function in society from the leader's list. When the team or pair has that numbered item listed on their sheet, they are asked to "Cover It" with a small paper chip or square.

5. At the end of the list, the teams that have all eight boxes covered with squares of paper or chips, call out "Cover It!" They are the winners.

FOLLOW-UP

Discuss the following with your students:

- How did you decide what was most important to keep in your life?
- Would you change your mind now on any of the items?
- Share what makes some of these items important to you.

Cover It Items Leader's List
(*Most important to having a good life and only ones called out)

9.	*Patience	11.	New Car
3.	*Kindness	12.	New Clothes
6.	*Love	13.	New House
5.	*Gentleness	4.	Diamond Ring
15.	*Happiness	14.	Air Jordan Shoes
10.	*Peacefulness	20.	Winning Team
17.	*Honor	22.	New Toy
19.	*Respect	23.	Favorite Television Show
7.	*Family	8.	Games
24.	*Talent	1.	Trip to Disney World
21.	*Good Health	2.	Favorite Food
18.	*Human Beings	16.	Candy

Cover It Items Student's List

1. A trip to Disney World

2. My favorite food

3. Kindness

4. A diamond ring

5. Gentleness

6. Love

7. Family

8. Games

9. Patience

10. Peacefulness

11. A new car

12. New clothes

13. A new house

14. Air Jordan shoes

15. Happiness

16. Candy

17. Honor

18. Human life

19. Respect

20. Winning team

21. Good health

22. New toy

23. A favorite television show

24. Talent

NASTY NOODLE

Grade Levels: K-5

Time: 30 Minutes

PURPOSE
To encourage positive thinking, viewing and actions.

MATERIALS NEEDED
Cooked spaghetti noodles
Spoon
Nasty Noodle Cards (reproduced & cutout)
Varied food ingredients (represents negative thinking)

OBJECT
To add distasteful ingredients to a
bowl of spaghetti to represent
negative thinking.

PROCEDURES

1. Define positive thinking as thoughts we have or statements we say to ourselves that encourage us, such as "All right!" or "Go for it!" Define negative thinking as thoughts we have or statements we say to ourselves that discourage us such as "I'm no good," or "It won't work."

2. Use the boiled spaghetti noodles to represent a person's brain or mind. Compile different ingredients to represent negative thinking.

3. Mix the Nasty Noodle Positive and Negative Cards together and place them in a stack. Ask students to draw a card from the stack. If the card drawn represents negative thinking, that person gets to add a "negative thinking" ingredient to the noodle mix. As things are added to the mix, discuss what negative thinking does to our minds.

4. If the card drawn represents positive thinking, give a treat to the person drawing the positive card.

FOLLOW-UP

Discuss the following with your students:

- What does negative thinking look like in our pot? How do you think it feels?
- What type of negative thinking do you use most often? How could you change?
- What type of positive thinking do you use most often? How do you feel about it?
- If you hear someone say negative statements about you, how can you change the negative statements into positive ones?

Nasty Noodle Positive Thinking Cards

Nasty Noodle Positive Thinking Cards **I'll try.**	Nasty Noodle Positive Thinking Cards **I can.**
Nasty Noodle Positive Thinking Cards **I'm good at that.**	Nasty Noodle Positive Thinking Cards **I want to.**
Nasty Noodle Positive Thinking Cards **I won't forget.**	Nasty Noodle Positive Thinking Cards **This is challenging.**
Nasty Noodle Positive Thinking Cards **This is going to be fun.**	Nasty Noodle Positive Thinking Cards **I'll do better next time.**

Nasty Noodle Positive Thinking Cards

I hope this is right.

Nasty Noodle Positive Thinking Cards

It will be O.K.

Nasty Noodle Positive Thinking Cards

This is my best work.

Nasty Noodle Positive Thinking Cards

I'm going to calm down and think.

Nasty Noodle Positive Thinking Cards

I will.

Nasty Noodle Positive Thinking Cards

Right on!

Nasty Noodle Positive Thinking Cards

I will study hard.

Nasty Noodle Positive Thinking Cards

I'll practice a lot.

Nasty Noodle Negative Thinking Cards

Nasty Noodle Negative Thinking Cards	Nasty Noodle Negative Thinking Cards
I can't.	**I can't do anything.**
I won't.	**Nobody likes me.**
I forgot.	**Everybody picks on me.**
My homework is no good.	**Everybody hates me.**

Nasty Noodle Negative Thinking Cards

I hate school.

Nasty Noodle Negative Thinking Cards

It's not my fault.

Nasty Noodle Negative Thinking Cards

I don't have
any friends.

Nasty Noodle Negative Thinking Cards

It's his/her
fault.

Nasty Noodle Negative Thinking Cards

I don't care.

Nasty Noodle Negative Thinking Cards

I give up.

Nasty Noodle Negative Thinking Cards

Whatever.

Nasty Noodle Negative Thinking Cards

Not me.

SHOOT THE HOOP

Grade Levels: K-5

Time: 30 Minutes

PURPOSE

To help students brainstorm character-building traits.

MATERIALS NEEDED

Portable basketball hoop
Soft squeeze ball
Paper
Pencil

OBJECT

To name a positive character trait
and shoot a basket to get points.

PROCEDURES

1. Divide the students into small teams of 4 or 5.

2. Give the students 5 minutes to brainstorm positive character-building traits and write these down. Define positive character-building traits as those characteristics which would make a better person, someone you'd want to be friends with, or someone whom you could trust. Examples include being honest, studying hard, being respectful, etc. Encourage the students to think of as many as they can.

3. For each positive character trait the team comes up with, the team gets one shot to make a basket using a small squeeze ball. Team members take turns shooting the basket.

4. Each successful shot is worth one or two points (leader's choice). The team who wins is the team that gets the most points for their shots.

FOLLOW-UP

Center discussion around the benefits of positive character-building traits. Ask students to consider "what's in it for them" if they act in this manner. Ask students to write down one character-building trait they would personally like to work on and formulate a plan for developing this trait.

MEDIA MUSH

Grade Levels: 4-5

Time: (2) 30 Minute Sessions

PURPOSES

To discuss lies we see in the media and how they influence our lives.
To begin looking carefully at the messages sent to us from the media
and the values those messages portray.

MATERIALS NEEDED

Advertisements from newspapers, magazines
Envelopes
Paper
Pen
Scissors

OBJECT

To get the most points by correctly
matching commercials, false truths
and real truths.

PROCEDURES

1. Cut out pictures of advertisements and write a description on tagboard. Laminate. Examples of descriptions:

   a. People drinking and eating in a van with a lot of friends, having a lot of fun.

   b. Your brain is like an egg. This is what happens when you're on drugs - the egg fries.

   c. The Tidy Bowl® Man.

   d. The Nestea® plunge.

   e. Starburst®.

2. After each picture, ask the students what the commercial implies. (For example, "If you drink beer, you'll have lots of friends and have lots of fun.")

3. Is the message depicting the truth or an illusion? If it is an illusion (as is the example above), what is the underlying truth? (For example, "If you drink too much, alcohol will damage your body, impair your ability to drive, impair your judgment, etc.")

4. After discussing a few examples with the whole group, divide the students into small groups, ask them to take four commercials and make a chart with the following titles:

Commercials	Implications & False Truths	Real Truths

5. Ask groups to write each answer from the three categories on separate sheets of paper so that each group ends up with 12 slips of paper (4 commercials times 3 categories).

6. Put these slips of paper in an envelope, number the envelopes and the chart with a preassigned number. Gather all the envelopes and the chart from students.

7. Distribute the envelopes to different groups and instruct them to match the commercials with the false truth and the real truths answers. Ask the group to raise their hands when they have completed the task. Check the matching answers with the correct chart.

8. Give each team one point for each correct answer.

9. The team with the most points wins.

VARIATION

Other categories for the teams to chart:

- Target Audience (For whom is the commercial intended?)
- Commercial's message
- How message was delivered (appeal to senses, sex appeal, greed, etc.)
- Purpose of the commercial or message

FOLLOW-UP

1. Talk about the kind of lies most people believe.

    - I must wear Calvin Klein® jeans.
    - I must have Nike Air® sneakers.
    - I need Bugle Boy® clothes.
    - I must drink to have friends and to have fun.

2. What would happen if each of us told 10 lies each day?

3. Are all lies wrong or bad? Give an example to defend your point of view.

OPERATION

Grade Levels: K-4

Time: 40 Minutes

PURPOSES

To teach students positive character-building strategies.

To teach students how different parts of the body affect other parts.

To teach students how what we do affects the way other people treat us.

MATERIALS NEEDED

Life size drawing of the body
Removable body parts
Operation Cards (reproduced & cutout)
Play money
Timer
Operation Second Cards (reproduced & cutout)

OBJECT

To win the most money by successfully completing the operation in the allotted amount of time.

PROCEDURES

1. Draw a life size picture of human body.

2. Make body parts so that they can be taken off the body and placed back on the body. You may want to laminate the parts and the body so that they can be used again. Outline each part on the whole body drawing. On the back of each body part, write the following questions:

2 eyes:	When you see someone hitting your friend, what do you do?
	When you see someone who looks very lonely, what do you do?
2 ears:	When you hear someone gossiping about your friend, what do you do?

	When you hear someone calling your mom a fat pig, what do you do?
1 mouth:	What are two good things you could say about someone to build them up?
1 nose:	When someone wants you to sniff cocaine, what do you say to them?
2 hands:	What are four things you could do to help someone with your hands?
	What are four things that could hurt someone with your hands that you need to avoid?
2 arms:	How could you be strong in a fighting situation without hitting someone?
	If you were a really strong person, what would you do if someone were talking about your best friend?
1 heart:	What are five ways to let your parents know you love them?
2 shoulders:	What are two ways to help your friend if they seem worried about something?
	What is one thing to do if you are concerned that your parents are stressed out?
1 stomach:	What are two good things to put in your stomach and two bad things to put in your stomach?
1 liver:	What are two reasons why alcohol is not good for you?
1 set of lungs:	What are two reasons why smoking is not good for you?
2 legs:	What are two good things you can do with your legs for exercise?
	What are two fun things you can do without drinking or smoking?
2 feet:	Where are two places you could go to learn something?
	What are two ways you can help people with your feet?
1 brain:	What are five good things you can think of to make you successful?

3. Divide the students into two teams.

4. Tell the students that this body has many troubles which need to be worked out. The class will need to give the body an "operation" to repair all of its parts. To do this, each student will have to become a specialist and describe a solution to the problem written on the back of the body part. Once the repair is complete, the part can be placed back on the large body. Tell the class that they have a certain amount of time to complete the task (20 to 60 seconds). This will be according to the Operation Second Card.

5. Place the names of the body parts in a makeshift doctor's bag. Choose a student to draw a body part card out of the bag.

6. Place several Operation Second Cards in another bag. After the student has drawn a body part, ask them to draw out an Operation Second Card. This card indicates the total amount of time allotted for this operation. The student has this amount of time to answer the question on the back of the body part chosen and place it back on the body. The goal for the group is to operate on the entire body before time runs out.

7.   If the student successfully completes the operation, give them $100 in play money. If the student does not complete the operation, they do not get the money.

8.   The winning team is the team that has collected the most money.

VARIATION

Ask a volunteer student to come to the front of the room. As the other students read the body part questions and answer them, place a sticker or small bandage on the student volunteer to indicate a successful operation. The sticker or bandage could be placed on or by the volunteer's heart if that body part card is answered correctly. The object is to have a sticker on or near each body part of the volunteer.

FOLLOW-UP

Discuss the following with your students:
- How are our bodies like this body?
- How do our decisions in real life affect our body?
- How does what we put in our stomach affect our brains?
- How does what we think in our brains affect our hands?
- How does what we do with our bodies affect the way other people treat us?
- How does what we do with our hearts affect the way our mouth works?

OPERATION SECOND CARDS
(MAKE 2 SETS)

Operation Second Cards	Operation Second Cards
15 **seconds**	**40** **seconds**
Operation Second Cards	Operation Second Cards
20 **seconds**	**45** **seconds**
Operation Second Cards	Operation Second Cards
25 **seconds**	**50** **seconds**

© 1997 by YouthLight, Inc.

Operation Second Cards

30 seconds

Operation Second Cards

55 seconds

Operation Second Cards

35 seconds

Operation Second Cards

60 seconds

OPERATION CARDS

Operation Cards

Left Eye

Operation Cards

Right Shoulder

Operation Cards

Heart

Operation Cards

Right Ear

Operation Cards

Right Eye

Operation Cards

Stomach

Operation Cards

Left Shoulder

Operation Cards

Mouth

Operation Cards

Left Ear

Operation Cards

Lungs

Operation Cards

Nose

Operation Cards

Right Foot

Operation Cards

Right Eye

Operation Cards

Stomach

Operation Cards

Right Leg

Operation Cards

Left Arm

Operation Cards

Left Hand

Operation Cards

Left Foot

Operation Cards

Left Leg

Operation Cards

Right Arm

Operation Cards

Right Hand

Operation Cards

Brain

Section VI:

FRIENDSHIP

While friends do not take the place of caring adults, parents, and teachers, friendships are a nurturing part of every student's experience. Students have the need both to reach out to others and be reached by them in return. The give and take of friendships also involves recognizing positive and negative relationships. These relationships often influence behavioral, academic, and social choices creating peer pressure that is often difficult to deal with. Students struggle daily with relationship choices and struggle to maintain friendships. This struggle is often the difference between having a positive or negative feeling about school as well as friends.

The personal needs of students change and grow depending on the positive interaction of friends. It is important for students to recognize their needs, realize how to make friends, know when it's important to leave friends, and understand when it's important to make their own decisions based on what they believe is right. The activities in this section examine these important choices and help students learn the art of friendship.

STICK TOGETHER

Grade Levels: 1-5

Time: 30 Minutes

PURPOSE

To help students identify positive characteristics that teach them when to stick together with friends and when it's best not to stick with them.

MATERIALS NEEDED

Stick Together Cards (reproduced & cutout)
Masking Tape

OBJECT

To get taped together for correctly identifying positive and negative characteristics, and walk without breaking the tape.

PROCEDURES

1. Put the Stick Together Cards in a basket. Explain that some cards describe traits that help friends stick together, such as sharing or helping, whereas some cards describe traits that pull friends apart, such as gossiping or jealousy.

2. Ask one student at a time to choose a card out of the basket.

3. Ask the student to identify whether the trait is a "sticking together" trait or a "pulling apart" trait. If the trait is a sticking together trait, ask the student to stand up and place his/her arms in the air. Wrap masking tape around the student's waist, and ask the student to lower his/her arms.

4. Call other students to choose a card. Each time a positive trait is drawn, ask the student to

stand beside the taped student as you tape this student to the previous student. (This usually works better if every other student faces in opposite directions.)

5. Play continues until seven or eight students are taped together. Ask the students to walk together to a predetermined destination. They must walk without breaking the tape. If they are able to work together to accomplish this goal, they are declared winners.

6. Begin play again with other students taking turns.

FOLLOW-UP

Take the opportunity to suggest that as long as the group is doing appropriate things, then it is O.K. to stick with this group. However, if someone steals, seriously hurts someone, or cheats on tests, then you should break away or pull apart from the group. Discuss the difficulty of pulling away from friends due to tremendous peer pressure.

When the seven or eight students return from their goal challenge, discuss the above concept. Ask the first student what they would do if the rest of their group decided to take drugs. The student may say "break away" from them. Ask the student to then symbolically break the tape. Ask this student to find other friends. Teach students that it may be more difficult to stay true to this decision if they stay alone, and encourage them to choose other friends who are engaging in positive behaviors.

At some point, the tape may break. When the kids look at you for what to do, discuss mending friendships, the importance of apologies and accepting responsibility when things go wrong. Piece the tape back together; caution that friendships are often more difficult to mend and children need to learn the importance of being careful with friends.

Stick Together Cards

Sticking Together Cards	Sticking Together Cards
sharing	**hitting**
"You're a kind person."	**"You're nice."**
helping	**fighting**
"You're a nerd."	**"You're stupid."**

Sticking Together Cards

gossiping

Sticking Together Cards

helping to pick
up someone's
books

Sticking Together Cards

"You're a
great friend."

Sticking Together Cards

"You're the best."

Sticking Together Cards

pinching

Sticking Together Cards

rolling your eyes

Sticking Together Cards

"You're too fat."

Sticking Together Cards

talking to someone
if they're sad

© 1997 by YouthLight, Inc.

Sticking Together Cards	Sticking Together Cards
touching inappropriately	**talking to someone if they're mad**
Sticking Together Cards	Sticking Together Cards
"I don't like your mom."	**giving a pat on the back**
Sticking Together Cards	Sticking Together Cards
hugging	**talking badly about someone's mom**
Sticking Together Cards	Sticking Together Cards
helping with homework	**burping**

Sticking Together Cards

**always begging
for food**

Sticking Together Cards

taking turns

Sticking Together Cards

stealing

Sticking Together Cards

sharing snacks

Sticking Together Cards

**loyalty to
friends**

Sticking Together Cards

**inviting people
to a party**

Sticking Together Cards

**protecting your
friend's reputation**

Sticking Together Cards

**inviting people
to play**

Sticking Together Cards

**tattling on
a friend**

Sticking Together Cards

**leaving people
out**

Sticking Together Cards

playing together

Sticking Together Cards

snatching the ball

Sticking Together Cards

**including others
when playing**

Sticking Together Cards

sharing a toy

Sticking Together Cards

refusing to gossip

Sticking Together Cards

helping others

SNOWMAN

Grade Levels: 2-5

Time: 30 Minutes

PURPOSE
To understand how actions can block out friendship.

MATERIALS NEEDED
Snowman Friendship Cards (reproduced & cutout)
White trash bag
Construction paper parts
(eyes, nose, hat, mouth, snowballs, buttons)

OBJECT
To correctly determine whether a card
is a positive or negative quality
and make a snowman.

PROCEDURES

1. Choose a volunteer from the group. Put a large white plastic trash bag over the volunteer's head. Make sure the bag has holes for breathing already cut into it, and that head and arm holes have been cutout.

2. Ask members of the group to select a Snowman Friendship Card. Each card contains either positive or negative qualities of friendship building. Ask the student to decide if the quality on the card would block out friendship (you would not feel comfortable with that person), or build up a good friendship (you would feel comfortable with that person).

3. If the student answers correctly whether the quality is positive or negative, he/she tapes a snowman part to the student in the trash bag. See the materials section for the parts used which will eventually make a snowman.

VARIATION

Surprise the group by not telling the name of the game in advance. See if they can discover what is happening to the volunteer. If the snowman is to be a surprise, direct the student who is putting on the parts as to which part to put on.

FOLLOW-UP

Discuss the following with your students:

- Which positive friendship qualities do you practice with your friends?
- Which negative friendship qualities do you practice that can block out friendship?
- How does it feel not to have a friend?

POSITIVE SNOWMAN FRIENDSHIP CARDS

Positive Snowman Friendship Cards

HONESTY

Positive Snowman Friendship Cards

SHARING

Positive Snowman Friendship Cards

LOYALTY

Positive Snowman Friendship Cards

FUN-LOVING

Positive Snowman Friendship Cards

HAPPY

Positive Snowman Friendship Cards

GOOD LISTENING

Positive Snowman Friendship Cards

TRUSTWORTHY

Positive Snowman Friendship Cards

HELPFUL

272

Positive Snowman Friendship Cards

KIND

Positive Snowman Friendship Cards

RESPECTFUL

Positive Snowman Friendship Cards

GENTLE

Positive Snowman Friendship Cards

NICE

Positive Snowman Friendship Cards

PATIENT

Positive Snowman Friendship Cards

GOOD

WORKER

Positive Snowman Friendship Cards

WELL

MANNERED

Positive Snowman Friendship Cards

POLITE

NEGATIVE SNOWMAN FRIENDSHIP CARDS

Negative Snowman Friendship Cards

GOSSIP

Negative Snowman Friendship Cards

CALLS OTHERS NAMES

Negative Snowman Friendship Cards

FROWNS A LOT

Negative Snowman Friendship Cards

DOESN'T LISTEN

Negative Snowman Friendship Cards

MAKES FUN OF OTHERS

Negative Snowman Friendship Cards

BRAGS

Negative Snowman Friendship Cards

TATTLES

Negative Snowman Friendship Cards

SHOWS OFF

Negative Snowman Friendship Cards

TELLS LIES

Negative Snowman Friendship Cards

BOSSY

Negative Snowman Friendship Cards

IS ROUGH

Negative Snowman Friendship Cards

HAS AN ATTITUDE

(ROLLS EYES, SHRUGS SHOULDER)

Negative Snowman Friendship Cards

DISHONEST

Negative Snowman Friendship Cards

FIGHTS

Negative Snowman Friendship Cards

THREATENS

OTHERS

Negative Snowman Friendship Cards

PUSHES

OTHERS

FRIENDSHIP BRIDGE

Grade Levels: 1-5

Time: 30 Minutes

PURPOSE

To help students recognize the characteristics
needed to build good friendship.

MATERIALS NEEDED

Paper
Pens
Trays of blocks
Plastic drinking glasses
Other non-breakable items

OBJECT

To point out a favorable characteristic
of a good friend, then race with a friend
while balancing a tray (bridge)
to the finish.

PROCEDURES

1. Give qualities that are important for a good friend to have.

2. Ask the volunteer to come up to the front of the room and cite a characteristic that they think is most important to friendship. (Examples are: honesty, loyalty, happiness, sensitivity, trustworthiness.) If clues are needed, help develop their vocabulary.

3. Ask the class to show their approval or disapproval of the student's characteristics by putting their thumbs up if they agree that the characteristic is important, or by putting their thumbs down if they don't think the characteristic is important to building a good friendship. If the class determines that the characteristic is positive, write the characteristic on the board, on paper, or on a card that can be taped to the person who gave the characteristic.

4. The student who has volunteered a positive characteristic chooses a friend to come up front with them. As each pair comes up, they form two parallel lines by facing each other and clasping hands around wrists: This is the Friendship Bridge.

5. Challenge each pair to balance a tray of blocks, plastic glasses, or other unbreakable items on their arms while they race the clock to see if they can get to another part of the room without knocking anything off of the tray. Depending upon the size of the classroom, pairs should race one at a time. Ask for more volunteers as time allows.

VARIATION

Do a trust fall. Build four bridges of friendship by clasping wrists. Let one student fall backwards. Emphasize trust and what happens if we let each other down.

FOLLOW-UP

Discuss the following with your students:
- What are some qualities that you would like to work on?
- Why is it important to build friendship bridges?
- How did you and your friend work together in the timed race?
- What would have helped you and your friend do better?

FRIENDLY FLIP OUT

Grade Levels: 2-5

Time: 30 Minutes

PURPOSE
To teach students things that will block out friendship.

MATERIALS NEEDED
Friendly Flip Out Cards (reproduced & cutout)
Two small friend boards
Blocks to cover each board
One die

OBJECT
To get as many points as possible from the Friendly Flip Out Cards without having your board blocked out.

PROCEDURES

1. Make two small boards with pictures of friends either drawn or cutout from magazines which cover the entire board. Use construction paper which has been laminated after the pictures of friends have been placed on it.

2. Cut out a number of squares which, when all are placed on the board, completely cover the board. This number should be the same for both boards. To begin, set the squares aside.

3. Divide the class into two teams.

4. Choose one team member to begin the game. Roll the die. This team member draws this number of cards from a stack of Friendly Flip Out Cards. Some of these cards depict situations that help friendship, some that block out friendship. The cards that are positive have points

on them. If the card chosen is positive, the team is able to keep these cards and add up the points at the end of the game. If the card chosen is negative, the team has to take a square and block out a segment on the board. For example, the team member draws the following cards:

Sharing + 5
*Hitting   [place one square on the board]
*Stepping on toes   [place another square on the board]
Hugging + 3
Helping + 2

The team would have placed two squares on the board and banked 10 points.

5. Play continues until the boards are blocked out or time is called by the leader. The winner is determined by adding the total number of positive points.

VARIATION

Take off the block segments on the pictures if the card is positive. Let the team determine if it is negative or positive. The winner is the one who has the fewest number of block segments to friend-ship on the pictures.

FOLLOW-UP

Focus discussion on things that prevent students from being your friends, as well as things that enhance friendship. Ask students to brainstorm ideas to enhance friendship. Establish a bragging time in which students can brag on things others have done to be helpful or kind. Each student who has been a good friend gets a prize of some sort.

FRIENDLY FLIP OUT CARDS

Friendly Flip Out Cards	Friendly Flip Out Cards
sharing **5**	**walking quietly** **3**
hugging **3**	**being gentle** **4**
picking up books **3**	**being kind** **4**
helping the other students **3**	**being sweet to friends** **3**

Friendly Flip Out Cards	Friendly Flip Out Cards
helping your friend with school work **4**	**being respectful** **5**

Friendly Flip Out Cards	Friendly Flip Out Cards
working hard **5**	**taking card of your friend's property** **3**

Friendly Flip Out Cards	Friendly Flip Out Cards
being honest **5**	**being kind** **4**

Friendly Flip Out Cards	Friendly Flip Out Cards
helping the other students **3**	**helping your friend clean up** **4**

Friendly Flip Out Cards

telling your friend
nice things
5

Friendly Flip Out Cards

not leaving
people out
4

Friendly Flip Out Cards

being clean
2

Friendly Flip Out Cards

not pulling hair
3

Friendly Flip Out Cards

combing your hair
2

Friendly Flip Out Cards

not hitting
3

Friendly Flip Out Cards

studying hard
3

Friendly Flip Out Cards

not sticking out
your tongue
3

Friendly Flip Out Cards

being polite
4

Friendly Flip Out Cards

loving people
5

Friendly Flip Out Cards

being nice
3

Friendly Flip Out Cards

being patient
4

Friendly Flip Out Cards

not gossiping
4

Friendly Flip Out Cards

being kind
3

Friendly Flip Out Cards

gossiping

Friendly Flip Out Cards

telling someone they
smell like a dumpster

© 1997 by YouthLight, Inc.

Friendly Flip Out Cards

laughing at others

Friendly Flip Out Cards

telling someone
they eat roaches

Friendly Flip Out Cards

calling someone
a fat pig

Friendly Flip Out Cards

telling someone they
look like a cow

Friendly Flip Out Cards

calling someone
a hog

Friendly Flip Out Cards

pulling hair

Friendly Flip Out Cards

calling someone
a nerd

Friendly Flip Out Cards

stepping on toes

Friendly Flip Out Cards

**calling someone
a dog face**

Friendly Flip Out Cards

cheating

Friendly Flip Out Cards

**telling someone they
have dog breath**

Friendly Flip Out Cards

**calling someone
bird brain**

Friendly Flip Out Cards

**calling someone
baldie**

Friendly Flip Out Cards

**calling someone
blondie**

Friendly Flip Out Cards

**calling someone
weirdo**

Friendly Flip Out Cards

**calling someone
barky**

Friendly Flip Out Cards	Friendly Flip Out Cards
calling someone chicken	**hitting**
Friendly Flip Out Cards	Friendly Flip Out Cards
calling someone smart aleck	**stealing**
Friendly Flip Out Cards	Friendly Flip Out Cards
calling someone wimp	**cursing**
Friendly Flip Out Cards	Friendly Flip Out Cards
calling someone idiot	**pushing**

Friendly Flip Out Cards

calling someone
coo-coo

Friendly Flip Out Cards

pinching

FRIENDSHIP FOLLIES

Grade Levels: 1-5

Time: 30 Minutes

PURPOSE

To help students get to know each other and to work on listening skills.

MATERIALS NEEDED

Tokens

OBJECT

To remember what others' answers were and receive a token.

PROCEDURES

1. Divide the students into small teams of four or five people.

2. Choose one person from each group to be the team leader for the first round.

3. Create your own questions or choose from the following:

   What is your favorite ice cream?

   What is your favorite toy?

   Where would you like to go on vacation?

   What is your favorite food?

   What is your favorite holiday?

   Where do you like to go to eat?

   What is your favorite sport?

4. Choose one of these questions to ask the team leader. The team leader will find out the answer to the questions from each of their team members. Instruct the team leader to raise their hand when this task is completed.

5. Ask the team leader to share the team's answers with the entire class.

6. Have tokens ready to provide each group for being on task, listening to others speak, being quiet when instructed to do so, etc.

7. Once the team leader finishes sharing each of their team members' answers, use the tokens to check for listening skills. For example, if the question was "What is your favorite ice cream?" ask if anyone in the class could remember a team member's response. For each response correctly matched to a student, the student gets a token. Instruct the class that all tokens received belong to the team as a whole. You may also ask other questions. The game may go something like this:

Student	Responses to Questions
Joe	chocolate
Mary	vanilla
Sue	orange
John	pecan
Bill	cherry

First set of questions: Students are asked to remember what flavors others like. For example, one student remembers that Mary likes vanilla ice cream. This student is awarded one token.

Second set of questions: "Who remembers which teammate likes orange ice cream?" Award a token if someone guesses Sue.

Third set of questions: Ask if anyone can remember what flavor Bill likes. Award a token if someone answers cherry.

The number of tokens awarded can be increased on the second and third sets of questions.

8. Next, choose new team leaders as well as new questions. Again, the team leader finds out the answers from the group and shares them with the class. Play continues for several questions or as time permits.

9. Those teams with the most tokens win.

FOLLOW-UP

Focus discussion on how to make friends as well as how important it is to truly listen to others as they are sharing about themselves. Other interesting things will arise during the discussions. For example, there may only be one student in the room who likes a particular thing and fifteen students who like the same thing. Discuss the importance of standing alone in tough decisions. Mention that we all have similarities and differences; the secret lies in trying to find similarities and make friends among all different kinds of people.

HOPSCOTCH HAPPENINGS

What is your
favorite color?

Grade Levels: K-4

Time: 30 Minutes

PURPOSE

To teach students to affirm themselves and others.
To help students get to know each other.

MATERIALS NEEDED

Hopscotch boards (made from landscaping plastic)
Happenings Ball

OBJECT

To answer questions while trying to reach
the end of the hopscotch board.

PROCEDURES

1. Make a hopscotch board out of landscaping plastic with the appropriate blocks made from contact paper. Make enough hopscotch boards to correspond with the number of groups that will be playing.

2. Make the Happenings Ball by following the patterns on page 293-294. Make enough balls for each group. The ball will have 12 sides, each side having a question written on it.

3. Divide the group into small groups of 3 or 4. This game is best played with 1 or 2 small groups.

4. Play the game exactly like hopscotch, with the following exception: instead of throwing a rock during their turn, students will throw the Happenings Ball. One question will appear on top. To advance on the hopscotch board, the student must answer the question which appears on top. A sample game: Student #1 throws the Happenings Ball on square #1. If the ball lands in the first square, the student answers the question on top and hops over the entire

board. Student #2 then throws the ball to square #1 and answers the question on top of the Happenings Ball. Play continues with students trying to throw the ball to square #2, then square #3, etc. During each turn, students answer one question. If a question comes up that they have previously answered, they do not have to answer, and may go ahead and hop.

5.   If the ball doesn't land on the appropriate number, the student forfeits their turn, then returns to this same number when it is their turn again.

6.   Play ends when one student completes throwing the ball to the last number on the board. This student is declared the winner.

VARIATION

Instruct student to throw the ball to any number on the hopscotch board, answer the question and hop over the board. Continue until time is called. Declare no winner.

FOLLOW-UP

Focus discussion on how easy it is to get to know one another while doing fun things. These questions represent general ways of getting to know other people. Encourage students to make new friends by finding out general things about people. Sometimes there will be similarities, sometimes differences between them. Encourage students to find out these qualities and begin making new friends.

Directions for Making the Happenings Ball

1. Duplicate pages 293 - 294. Thick colored paper works best both for appearance and durability .

2. Cut out ball shapes.

3. Fold all outer edges inward so that a crease is formed. Turn the edges back out to the regular ball shape. This is where the ball pieces will be connected.

4. Begin with one ball shape. Glue one edge of each of five different balls to the five edges of the one ball shape. You now have six balls connected together by five edges. Make sure the creased edges are connected to that they fold outward on the ball shape - not inward.

5. Connect the five balls to each other by gluing the middle edges together. You will now have three total edges of each individual form glued together. This should form half of a ball.

6. Repeat procedure 4 & 5 with the remaining six shapes.

7. Connect the two ball halves together by connecting the two bottom edges of each of the five pieces of the first ball to the two bottom edges of the five pieces from the other ball.

8. You now should have a fully formed ball with all edges turned outward.

Happenings Ball

What is your favorite color?

Where is your favorite place to go?

What is your favorite food?

What is your favorite pet?

How many brothers & sisters do you have?

What is your favorite subject in school?

What is your favorite game?

What do you want to be when you grow up?

What is your favorite holiday?

What is your favorite season?

What is your favorite ice cream?

What is your favorite toy?

Section VII:

Self-Esteem

The term, self-esteem, is sometimes misunderstood. Self-esteem is often believed to be the special feelings a person holds about him/herself. Actually, self-esteem has a much broader base and only begins with feelings of self-worth. It further includes a person's ability to get along with others, to reach goals, and to help others. Without these abilities, feelings of self-worth quickly fade away. To have positive self-esteem, it is essential to develop these abilities.

Self-esteem cannot be given to another, but can be easily damaged and taken away. Increasing students' awareness of areas in which they are unique, special, and worthy helps them to heal or repair any damaged parts of their self-esteem. Many times, students compare themselves to others and feel lacking. Helping them to discover their strengths through small accomplishments plants the seed for further growth and development.

The activities in this section focus on building self-esteem through focusing on the student and the student's ability to interact with other people, a crucial component of self-esteem. Some activities look for students' personal strengths and encourage positive movement towards goals. Combined, the activities seek to promote overall positive self-esteem among students.

JENGA® JIVE

Grade Levels: 1-5

Time: 30 Minutes

PURPOSE

To teach students to make affirming comments to each other and work together.

MATERIALS NEEDED

Jenga®

OBJECT

To answer the questions without making the blocks fall.

PROCEDURES

1. Using the Jenga® game (available in toy stores), invite a small group of students to play the game as the directions indicate.

2. However, before each student's turn, ask them to compliment another student by stating something they like about the student, something the student does well in class, or something helpful the student did for the speaking student.

3. Play continues until the blocks fall.

APPROPRIATE GROUPS TO USE THE GAME WITH:

- ADHD children to encourage self-control and concentration
- Aggressive children to encourage cooperation
- Gossiping children to encourage them to talk positively

FOLLOW-UP

Center the discussion on working together to make others feel special or good about themselves. Just like the Jenga® blocks must maintain a delicate balance to continue standing, so friendships require good care to maintain a positive balance.

If You're Happy

Grade Levels: K-5

Time: 30 Minutes

PURPOSES

To enhance positive self-esteem, practice listening skills,
and utilize self-control.

MATERIALS NEEDED

Soft squeeze ball

OBJECT

To catch the ball, disclose a favorite thing,
then throw the ball to someone else.

PROCEDURES

1. Ask each student to sit on top of his/her desk.

2. Begin by telling students what makes you happy such as something, someone, or an activity at home, at school, or in the community. Then throw the soft squeeze ball to a student.

3. The student who catches the ball then tells what makes them happy, trying not to repeat what has already been said, and then throws the ball to someone else.

4. No one may talk while another person has the ball. If they do, they must sit down in their chairs until another person disobeys the silent rule and has to sit down. When this happens, the previous offender may get back up.

5. Also, if a student does not catch the ball or throws the ball badly so the person can't get at the ball, that student needs to sit down.

Note: Only one person sits down at a time, and a person can get back up as soon as some one else has to sit down.

VARIATION

Throw the ball to other people and repeat what the person before you said before giving your favorite things.

FOLLOW-UP

Discuss the following with your students:
- What did you learn about others that you didn't know before?
- How did you feel about sharing happy information with others?
- Did it help you to begin to make other choices about helping yourself to be happy? How will you do this?

CRATER CROSS

Grade Levels: K-5

Time: 30 Minutes

PURPOSE
To help students affirm each other.

MATERIALS NEEDED
Laminated paper craters
Sand timer

OBJECT
To cross the river and step only on the craters while a teammate says positive things about you.

PROCEDURES

1. Make craters out of pieces of paper or use old crates.

2. Divide students into two teams. Ask teams to go to opposite sides of the room. Place eight or nine craters between the two teams.

3. Choose one student to cross the river on the craters. The student has to step on each of the craters as he/she crosses the river.

4. Position the child on the first crater and turn the sand timer over. During this time period, the moving student must choose a team member to say something positive or affirming to him/her before he/she can move to the next crater.

5. The student wins if he/she can cross the craters before the time runs out. The team is awarded 25 points for each child who crosses the river during the timed period.

6. The team with the most points wins.

VARIATION

Add a ball to make it more challenging. The "moving" student throws the ball to a team member from the crater. The team member who catches the ball must compliment the moving player. If either of the players drop the ball, the moving player must start again. This aspect encourages team cooperation and seems to make everyone pay better attention to the game.

FOLLOW-UP

Ask the students how it felt to affirm others and think positively about themselves during the activity. Ask students to commit to saying a certain number of statements about themselves or others during the next few days. To reinforce this, do other activities including writing in journals, playing the balloon bop, doing the mailbox activity, and others found in this book.

CLOSE ENCOUNTERS

Grade Levels: K-5

Time: 30 Minutes

PURPOSE
To help students to get to know each other.

MATERIALS NEEDED
Laminated paper with questions on them
Sand timer

OBJECT
To step on questions across the room,
answering them and getting
10 points for each.

PROCEDURES

1. Write questions on 10-14 Pieces of paper and laminate. For non-reading children, pictures can
    be placed on the cards. Questions could be as follows:

    a. What is your favorite ice cream?

    b. What is your favorite color?

    c. What is your favorite music group?

    d. What is your favorite toy?

    e. What is your favorite place to go?

    f. What is your favorite restaurant?

    g. What is your favorite sport?

    h. What is your favorite subject?

    I. What is a hobby that you have?

    j. What do you want to be when you grow up?

    k. If you had money to give away, who would you give it to? Why?

POWER PLAY

l. Who is one adult that you admire? Why?

m. What is one quality or characteristic you like to see in other people?

n. Name someone you think is successful.

2. Divide students into two teams. Ask each team to go to opposite sides of the room. Place pieces of laminated paper in a row in the center of the teams.

3. Choose one student to step across the papers. Set a one minute timer. The student must see how many questions they can step on and answer before time runs out. Award each question answered 10 points for the team.

4. Play continues with teams taking turns as time allows.

FOLLOW-UP

Discuss, with the students, how people get to know each other. Emphasize that this usually happens by asking people questions and finding out more about them. Discuss the importance of listening to others as opposed to talking too much about oneself. Friendships develop by finding similarities and common interests as well as learning from others about their special interest.

TALKING BEHIND YOUR BACK

Grade Levels: 2-5

Time: 30 Minutes

PURPOSE

To show students that they can write affirming comments literally "behind someone's back."

MATERIALS NEEDED

Construction paper
Tape
Markers

OBJECT

To give compliments to other children by writing on the papers on their backs.

PROCEDURES

1. Tape a piece of construction paper to each student's back.

2. Talk to the students about ground rules. These rules should include no put-downs or inappropriate comments allowed. Should a student choose to break any of these rules, they would automatically be suspended from the game.

3. Write several appropriate comments or phrases on the board to help with spelling and to help students begin to think of comments they could write. (Be sure markers being used will not bleed through the paper to avoid staining clothing.)

4. Ask the students to mingle around the room, writing positive comments on each other's backs.

5. Ask the students to stop once the game has gone on for a few minutes or once the students have had time to obtain several comments on the pieces of paper on their backs. Ask them to sit in a circle.

6. Once the students are in a circle with paper still taped to their backs, randomly ask a student for a number between one and ten.

7. The student chosen to begin is the "walking" student. Depending on the number chosen, the student would then count this many students around the circle, and read the paper on this student's back. For example, if six were chosen, the walking student would read the sixth student's paper. The "walking" student then takes the "sitting" student's place, the "sitting" student becomes the "walking" student.

VARIATION

Allow students to read their own paper or pair with another student for sharing.

FOLLOW-UP

Direct this game in a positive manner, ask students to discuss how they felt while playing. Students will usually answer positively and thus, they can be challenged to utilize this concept in the classroom. Challenge the class to tell you in a class meeting how someone affirmed them in some way during the week. Urge students to talk positively about their friends and classmates.

DUCK, DUCK, FRIEND

Grade Levels: K-3

Time: 30 Minutes

PURPOSE
To teach students how to affirm each other.

MATERIALS NEEDED
None

OBJECT
To run around the circle without being tagged by the chaser, while also giving compliments.

PROCEDURES

1. Ask students to sit in a circle. Choose one student to be "it." Tell students that it is important to let our friends know the positive things we think about each other.

2. The student who is "it" walks around the circle tapping each student on the head. As this student touches another student on the head, they say a compliment to the child whose head is being touched.

3. Whenever the student is ready to have someone chase him/her, he/she merely taps someone on the head and says "friend," then runs around the circle back to their friend's seat.

4. The child chosen as "friend" then gets up and chases the student around the circle back to the friend's seat. If the running student makes it around the circle without getting caught, the chasing student becomes "it." If the running student is caught, he/she must sit in the

mushpot (the center of the circle). If a student goes in the mushpot, the class can say together, "We love you," or some other appropriate comment.

VARIATION

Ask each student to draw a name of one student in the group. Each student is then asked to write a short secret letter about this student writing compliments and things they like about this person. One student is chosen to begin. This student walks around the circle saying "duck, duck,...friend" stopping at the person whose name they had chosen and dropping the letter behind him/her. The student can read their letter silently after the chase.

FOLLOW-UP

Focus discussion on the importance of affirmation in dealing with friends. Challenge students to begin saying these statements during classroom time and verbally reinforce them whenever they are heard saying positive statements.

I Can Do It

Grade Levels: K-5

Time: 30 Minutes

PURPOSE

To encourage students to draw things they are able
to do or are successful with.

MATERIALS NEEDED

Dice
Blackboard & Chalk

OBJECT

To win the most points by drawing
an activity that a team member can do.

PROCEDURES

1. Divide the group into two teams.

2. Determine which team can go first to throw the dice. The number thrown on the dice determines the number of the statement they are to respond to in drawing - no words. Note: Drawings must be different each time. See statements below:

    1. Draw a picture of one thing you do well.
    2. Draw a picture of one way you help at home.
    3. Draw a picture of one way you help your teacher.
    4. Draw a picture of your favorite subject.
    5. Draw a picture of something you're very proud of.
    6. Draw a picture of you doing something to make you a better person.
    7. Draw a picture of what you want to be when you grow up.
    8. Draw a picture of you and your friends doing something fun.
    9. Draw a picture of you saying no to drugs.
    10. Draw a picture of you working hard in school.

11. Draw a picture of you helping your friends in a tough situation.
12. Draw a picture of you helping someone.

3. Announce the statement and count down to zero. Let one member from that team call out "I can do it!" The one who is heard first by the leader gets one minute to do their picture on the chalkboard.

4. Let each team take turns guessing what the picture is, beginning with the team whose member drew the picture.

5. Give the points that were on the dice to the team when the team guesses the drawing.

VARIATIONS

1. Ask the students to make books of talents they have, ways to have good manners, ways to make friends, what they would like to be when they grow up, etc. Each student is responsible for one page which might become part of a book. This serves to help students feel good about themselves, learn about their friends, and become connected with the group. Each student either responds to the same statement or each student can answer a different statement.

2. This game can be played with only one individual.

3. Drawings may be placed on acetate overlays for use on the overhead projector.

FOLLOW-UP

Focus discussion on appreciating others' talents and taking time to understand people. Play guessing games with the information in the book, thus helping students feel important and valued in the classroom.

MUSICAL DRESS UP

Grade Levels: K-5

Time: 30 Minutes

PURPOSE

To help students learn to say positive things about themselves.

MATERIALS NEEDED

Large trash bag
"Silly" dress up items
Tape Player
Music

OBJECT

To quickly think of positive things to say about yourself or others and avoid dressing up.

PROCEDURES

1. Ask students to sit in a circle. As the music starts, pass the bag around the circle. When the music stops, the student has five seconds to say something positive about him/herself or someone else in the group. If they are unable to do it, they have to reach into the bag and put on whatever they pull out.

2. Students are declared winners at the end of the game if they have not had to "dress up."

VARIATION

Ask students specific questions and give them 5 seconds to answer. For example:

1. What is your favorite subject?
2. What is one thing you are good at?
3. What do you want to be when you grow up?
4. Name one way to help people.

FOLLOW-UP

Ask students how they can "think fast" throughout the day to prevent themselves from looking "silly" in front of their friends. Your discussion may focus on study habits, homework, peer pressure, or behavior. Help students realize they are often called upon to make "split second" decisions in each of these areas. The wrong decision may cause them to face an unpleasant consequence in front of peers, family, or teachers.

MUSICAL MOVES

Grade Levels: K-5

Time: 30 Minutes

PURPOSE

To teach students to give affirming statements to each other.

MATERIALS NEEDED

Musical tape
Tape player
Ball
Dice (for variation)

OBJECT

To think of compliments for other children and tell them within the allotted time period.

PROCEDURES

1. Ask students to sit in a circle. Tell students that they will get many gifts of compliments from other students by asking them to tell them something they do well.

2. Start the music and tell children to throw or roll the ball to each other.

3. Whenever the music stops, the student who is holding the ball has 10 seconds to choose three students to give them compliments or tell them something they do well. If a chosen student is unable to give the compliment in time, they are out of the game. (Note: Usually students are able to do this in plenty of time. However, if this seems to be a problem, extend the time a bit. The goal is for the children to be successful.)

4. Play continues as long as the leader desires.

VARIATION

To make the game more interesting, provide a list of questions. Prior to each round, the last student to hold the ball throws the dice to determine the question. Questions correspond to the number rolled on the dice. The questions are listed below:

1. What is one subject this person does really well in?
2. What is one sport this person excels in?
3. What is one quality you admire about this person?
4. What is one thing you like about this person?
5. What is one thing that makes this person a good student in class?
6. What is one thing you like about this person's face?
7. What is one thing that makes this person a good friend?
8. What is one caring thing you've seen this person do?
9. What is the best thing you can think of about this person?
10. What is the nicest thing you've ever seen this person do?
11. What is one thing this person does to make them smarter?

If the variation is used, the time may stay the same, but require only one person to answer as answers are more complicated and require more time. Play can continue as time allows.

FOLLOW-UP

Encourage students to quickly think of affirming responses. Ask the students to describe how they felt both giving compliments and having friends compliment them. This activity is designed to help the student learn to "think" fast in a positive manner about his/her friends.

MAGAZINE MADNESS SCAVENGER HUNT

Grade Levels: K-5

Time: 1 hour or 2-30 minute sessions

PURPOSE

To help students critically look for information that is beneficial to them.

MATERIALS NEEDED
Magazines
Poster paper
Scissors
Timer
Bag

OBJECT

To correctly guess which pictures correspond with questions on the list and obtain the most points.

PROCEDURES

1. Make a large board out of poster paper with 25 total squares. Place an index card or small piece of construction paper over half of each square to make a pocket or cut a library pocket in half and use the bottom half. Number each square beginning with one and ending with 25. See example below:

Pocket →

1	2	3	4	5
6	7	8	9	10
11	12	13	14	15
16	17	18	19	20
21	22	23	24	25

2. Give each student a magazine, scissors, and a copy of the list of statements on page 317. Assign each student a number on the list.

3. Give students a short amount of time to find the item requested on their list. Ask each student to cut out the word, phrase, or picture and collect these items by passing around a bag in which the students can save their items. Spot check these items as they are collected to make sure they reflect the assigned number. Ask students to place the number on the back of the picture.

4. Place each item collected randomly in a pocket on the board.

5. Divide students into two teams.

6. Ask each team to take turns choosing a number on the board, looking at the picture, word, or phrase in the pocket, and guessing which statement on the list this corresponds to. Set a timer for a small amount of time to expedite the game. If the team does not answer in the allotted amount of time, play goes to the other team. This team is given the opportunity to answer the same question in the allotted time frame. If the other team can answer, they win ten points for answering and are given their usual turn. For all answers you judge to be correct, the team is awarded 10 points. If the answer is incorrect, the team does not get any points and play goes to the other team. Many statements on the list are similar, therefore several pictures may refer to the same number. Use your own discretion.

7. Place extra points of 10, 20, 30, 40, or 50 points in various pockets to make the game more interesting.

8. Add an "extra" card to several pockets. This card is hidden from view and has the word "extra" written on it. When a student chooses a pocket with the extra card in it, the student has a chance to add an extra answer to the category for an additional 10 points. For example, if the student chooses a picture of a homeless person and answers that the picture refers to question 5 (a picture of someone you would not like to be like), they have a chance to describe someone else they may not want to be like.

9. Play continues as time allows. The winner is the team with the most points.

VARIATIONS

1.   Ask the students to make collages answering some of the questions and present the collage to the group.

2.   Divide the students into groups and ask them to find 3 or 4 answers to the statements. Ask the students to cut these out and share their findings with the group.

FOLLOW-UP

Focus discussion on what the students found, and what it would take to maintain the positive images found. Stress the importance of good education, good attitudes, good activities, etc. to make the students better people.

Magazine Madness Scavenger Hunt

1. One food to make you healthy.

2. One activity that is good for your heart.

3. One picture of something you'd like to be when you grow up.

4. One picture of something to help you succeed as an adult.

5. One picture of someone you would not like to be like.

6. One word that will help you be a better person.

7. Two titles of articles that will help you be a better person.

8. One picture of food that is not good for you.

9. One picture of ways kids can get in trouble.

10. One picture of teenagers in trouble.

11. One title of an article about a problem that kids might have.

12. One word telling a way to have fun without drugs.

13. One word telling a way to be successful in school.

14. One picture of an unsuccessful person.

15. One picture of a successful person.

16. One picture of something that is bad for you.

17. One picture of someone having fun without using drugs.

18. One picture of an unhealthy activity.

19. One picture of a good exercise.

20. One picture of a way to be smarter in school.

21. One word that would be a nice thing to say to someone.

22. One word that helps make friends.

23. One picture of a way to help someone.

24. One picture of a way to be kind.

25. One word describing a nice thing to do for someone.

LOOK AT THE STARS

Grade Levels: K-5

Time: 30 Minutes

PURPOSE
To enhance self-esteem.

MATERIALS NEEDED
Paper
Pencil

OBJECT
To collect as many stars as possible
to be stars of the class.

PROCEDURES

1. Have the students trace around their hand on a sheet of paper and write their name above the hand.

2. Call out different categories for which students can come to the front of the room. (A list is given on the page 320.) For example, if the leader says, "We're looking for stars who have dogs as pets," the stars may share the name of their dog or any other detail the leader wants to emphasize. If time allows, let the students who fit the certain category share something about that category.

3. Students who have been stars for a category then go back to their seats and make a star on their paper, or a small circle inside their drawn hand. Students draw a new star in their hand drawings for each time they get to be a star of the class.

4. At the end of the session ask students to count the number of stars or circles to see how many times they were a class star or important.

VARIATION

Use different feats instead of the attached list. Feats could include singing a favorite song, hopping on one foot for one minute, holding your breath for one minute, etc. Invite the students to try these feats in small groups and put down stars if the feat was accomplished.

FOLLOW-UP

Discuss the following with your students:

- How did you feel about being a star?
- For which category did you enjoy being a star? Why?
- What did you learn about some of your friends that you didn't know before?

LOOK AT THE STARS CATEGORIES

Come be a star if...

You have on tennis shoes

You have on something yellow

You have brown eyes

You have long hair

You have on shorts

You are wearing something on your head

You have a cat at home

You have a baby brother or sister

You have been to a zoo

You like spinach

You like football

You have to take out the trash at home

You can swim

You have flown on an airplane

You want to be a teacher

You have been to Disney World

You won a contest

THE LITTLE ENGINE THAT COULD

Grade Levels: K-5

Time: 30 Minutes

PURPOSE
To help students with self-motivation.

MATERIALS NEEDED
The Little Engine adapted review
Paper
Pencil
Timer with a second hand

OBJECT
To beat your time each time that the feat is attempted or repeated.

PROCEDURES

1. Review the story of The Little Engine.

2. Encourage students to try different timed feats to see if they can meet the challenge.

3. Ask students to accomplish a feat and record their own time. Encourage students to say to themselves, "I think I can."

4. Challenging feats to try:
    *   Jumps - one foot or both feet
    *   Jumping jacks
    *   The bicycle - hands on two adjoining desks, lifting the body with the arms while the feet make cycling motions not touching the floor

- Broad jump - mark starting and ending point with masking tape
- Sit-ups
- High jumps - measured by touching a point on the wall or door frame with masking tape
- Write a given sentence repeatedly to fill as much of the page as you can (Example: This is a great class to be proud of.)
- Do a simple math sheet to see how many problems can be done in a certain time
- Read a simple reading activity and answer questions.

(On the academic feats, the measure is quantity and not quality at this time.)

5. Focus discussion on trying to be the best you can be. Success comes, not just from competing, but from competing with one's self.

FOLLOW-UP

Discuss the following with your students:

- How did you feel accomplishing your feats?
- Which feat was the hardest, and which was the easiest for you?
- How did you feel when you beat the time on your challenge?
- How did you feel when you did not beat the time on your challenge?
- Would this help you in doing your schoolwork?

The Adapted Review of
The Little Engine That Could

Once upon a time, as you remember, there was a very little train engine that was asked to help another train engine that was broken down. The broken engine was taking a load of toys to the boys and girls who lived on the other side of the mountain. Two other engines, one a very big one and one a very fancy and shiny one, refused to help the broken engine.

The littlest engine said that he would try to help pull the broken engine over the mountain. It was a very steep and difficult mountain to get up, but each part of the way the littlest engine told himself, "I think I can, I think I can." He tried very hard, and he finally made it to the other side of the mountain. The littlest engine felt very happy with his great effort and also quite proud of his accomplishment.

All the way down the other side of the mountain the littlest engine told himself, "I thought I could, I thought I could." Telling himself these things helped him to achieve and put forth the effort in his challenge.

Section VIII:

Feelings

When an elementary age student can recognize and identify personal feelings and know that certain responses and reactions are the result of those feelings, their world can open up and they can be more aware of others' needs. Feelings of empathy, sympathy, and caring are thwarted if a student cannot deal with his/her own feelings. Knowing and recognizing acceptable and unacceptable responses to feelings can also lead a student to a more successful, emotionally healthy life.

The activities in this section look at basic feelings and help students learn to identify those feelings and how to communicate them to other people. It is also important for students to learn they can be in charge of their feelings by talking about them and by making plans to change their negative feelings to become positive. Behaviors often become the catalyst that help students turn those "frowns upside down." These strategies will be examined in this section with the ultimate goal of helping students grow in positive ways.

UPSIDE DOWN FROWN

Grade Levels: K-5

Time: 30 Minutes

PURPOSE

To encourage students to think of ways to help themselves choose to be happy.

MATERIALS NEEDED

Unhappy Situation Cards (reproduced & cutout)
Upside Down Frowns (reproduced & cutout)

OBJECT

To turn unhappy situations into happy ones and win Upside Down Frowns.

PROCEDURES

1. Divide students into two teams.

2. Instruct one team to act out an unhappy situation from an Unhappy Situation Card then challenge the other teams to come up with a solution that would help make someone happy in the unhappy situation.

3. If the challenged team gives a positive solution by changing the unhappy mood to a happy one, that team wins an upside down frown.

4. If the challenged team doesn't have a good solution, the team that acted out the situation may themselves give a happy solution to the unhappy situation and receive two upside down frown cards. Cards with no solutions should be repeated later.

5. The team who has the most Upside Down Frown Cards wins.

6. If neither team can think of a solution, you may give clues for solutions. (Examples: read, call a friend, draw, play with a friend, make something, work on a hobby, etc.)

FOLLOW-UP

Discuss the following with your students:

- Which activity would help you feel happier?
- Is it easier for you to be happy or sad? Why?
- What would help you choose to be happy?

UPSIDE DOWN FROWNS

Upside Down Frowns Upside Down Frowns Upside Down Frowns

Upside Down Frowns Upside Down Frowns Upside Down Frowns

UNHAPPY SITUATION CARDS

Unhappy Situation Cards	Unhappy Situation Cards
Your parents are getting a divorce.	School is boring.
Unhappy Situation Cards	Unhappy Situation Cards
Someone in your family is sick in the hospital.	Your pet just died.
Unhappy Situation Cards	Unhappy Situation Cards
Someone in your family died.	You are very sick.
Unhappy Situation Cards	Unhappy Situation Cards
Someone in your family is angry with you.	Someone uses drugs or alcohol in your home.

Unhappy Situation Cards

You have done something wrong, like stealing.

Unhappy Situation Cards

Your parents argue a lot and yell at each other.

Unhappy Situation Cards

The teacher doesn't like you.

Unhappy Situation Cards

Your parents call you bad names.

Unhappy Situation Cards

There is never anything to do at school.

Unhappy Situation Cards

A bully is picking on you.

Unhappy Situation Cards

Someone won't play with you

Unhappy Situation Cards

Someone calls you a name.

EMPTY THE STOCKING

Grade Levels: K-5

Time: 30 Minutes

PURPOSE

To learn vocabulary words for different feelings.

MATERIALS NEEDED

Feeling Cards (reproduced & cutout)
Spinner
Large envelope or Christmas stocking
Empty the Stocking Stimulus Situation List

OBJECT

To get rid of your feeling cards the fastest by deeming them appropriate for situations read by the group leader.

PROCEDURES

1. Review vocabulary words for feelings, selecting those words that would be appropriate for the grade level.

2. Divide the group into two teams.

3. Give each student three different feeling cards with vocabulary words on them, include a simple facial picture as a clue. These pictures can be found in <u>Games Children Should Play</u> by Cihak and Jackson-Heron[1]. In this book, there are 26 pictures of feelings. If this book is unavailable, you may use the Emptying the Stocking Feeling Cards alone.

[1]Cihak, Mary K., and Jackson, Barbara: <u>Games Children Should Play</u>. Scott Foresman and Company. Glenview, Illinois. 1980.

4. Read stimulus situations (from page 334) to the teams, such as, "When no one lets me play with them, I feel—."

5. Ask students to raise their hands if they have a card that lists an appropriate feeling to be used in that situation. Several different feelings may be applicable. Each student also must explain why they think a certain feeling would be a probable response.

6. Use a spinner to determine the number of responses to take from the teams. For example, if the spinner indicates a five, take cards from only five different students.

7. When a student gets rid of all of his/her cards, he/she gets a treat, or a point for his/her team (boys vs. girls, etc.)

8. Most of the time, there will be several winners at once. Allow play to continue by letting the winners get three more feeling cards out of a large envelope or Christmas stocking.

9. Tally the teams' scores and pronounce the team with the most points is the winner.

FOLLOW-UP

Discuss the following with your students:
- What made it difficult for you to decide what feeling was being portrayed in the situation?
- What made it easy for you to decide what feeling was being portrayed in the situation?
- What new feeling vocabulary did you learn?

EMPTY THE STOCKING STIMULUS SITUATIONS LIST

How would you feel if...?

...you had a birthday party

...your dog died

...you went to Disney World

...you got an A on a paper

...you got sent to the principal because you were in trouble

...your dad lost his job

...your parents got divorced

...you saw a glimmer under a rock

...you had a ball game and a birthday party and still had to do your homework that night

...your shirt tore at school

...your math class went on for two hours

...you had a science project due tomorrow and you hadn't started

...you had to talk to the whole 3rd and 4th grade classes about your project

...your best friend moved

...you stayed up too late last night

...someone stole your new pencil

...your grandmother was in the hospital

...you went to camp and were introducing yourself to new people

...you had a nightmare

...you just ate cookies and milk

...your best friend wouldn't speak to you

...you were taking a big test

...you were having a sleep-over

...you heard a noise late at night in your house

...your mom was having surgery

EMPTY THE STOCKING FEELING CARDS

(MAKE SEVERAL COPIES OF EACH CARD.)

Empty the Stocking Feeling Cards	Empty the Stocking Feeling Cards
Jealous	Happy
Empty the Stocking Feeling Cards	Empty the Stocking Feeling Cards
Curious	Rushed
Empty the Stocking Feeling Cards	Empty the Stocking Feeling Cards
Content	Embarrassed
Empty the Stocking Feeling Cards	Empty the Stocking Feeling Cards
Lonely	Shy

336

Empty the Stocking Feeling Cards	Empty the Stocking Feeling Cards
Hurt	Overwhelmed
Empty the Stocking Feeling Cards	Empty the Stocking Feeling Cards
Glad	Bored
Empty the Stocking Feeling Cards	Empty the Stocking Feeling Cards
Excited	Naughty
Empty the Stocking Feeling Cards	Empty the Stocking Feeling Cards
Tired	Kind

Empty the Stocking Feeling Cards

Frustrated

Empty the Stocking Feeling Cards

Energetic

Empty the Stocking Feeling Cards

Mad

Empty the Stocking Feeling Cards

Unhappy

Empty the Stocking Feeling Cards

Angry

Empty the Stocking Feeling Cards

Confident

Empty the Stocking Feeling Cards

Hopeful

Empty the Stocking Feeling Cards

Worried

338

Empty the Stocking Feeling Cards	Empty the Stocking Feeling Cards
Jolly	*Silly*
Empty the Stocking Feeling Cards	Empty the Stocking Feeling Cards
Fascinated	*Proud*
Empty the Stocking Feeling Cards	Empty the Stocking Feeling Cards
Worried	*Zany*
Empty the Stocking Feeling Cards	Empty the Stocking Feeling Cards
Ignored	*Friendly*

Empty the Stocking Feeling Cards

Tense

Empty the Stocking Feeling Cards

Restless

Empty the Stocking Feeling Cards

Discouraged

Empty the Stocking Feeling Cards

Satisfied

Empty the Stocking Feeling Cards

Loving

Empty the Stocking Feeling Cards

Scared

Empty the Stocking Feeling Cards

Bashful

Empty the Stocking Feeling Cards

Confused

POWER PLAY

Empty the Stocking Feeling Cards

Sad

Empty the Stocking Feeling Cards

Playful

Empty the Stocking Feeling Cards

Anxious

Empty the Stocking Feeling Cards

Helpful

Empty the Stocking Feeling Cards

Peaceful

Empty the Stocking Feeling Cards

Curious

Empty the Stocking Feeling Cards

Excited

Empty the Stocking Feeling Cards

Wiggly

TAKE A WALK

Grade Levels: K-5

Time: 30 Minutes

PURPOSE

To familiarize students with different feelings and their accompanying body language.

MATERIALS NEEDED

Two erasers or masking tape rolls

OBJECT

To walk exhibiting a predetermined emotion while balancing an object on your head and avoiding being tagged.

PROCEDURES

1. Divide the class into two teams.

2. Choose one member from each team to come up to the front of the class.

3. Ask each student to balance an object on their heads such as an eraser or masking tape roll.

4. Instruct students to "Take a Walk" around the room and exhibit the feeling you describe (see page 343). For example, they may need to walk sadly, happily, angrily, etc. A sad walk would be slower than a happy walk. Both students walk with the same feeling.

5. As each student "Takes a Walk" and shows the body language of a certain feeling, instruct one student to chase and tag the other. Decide in advance which student chases the other, such as the boy chases the girl. When the next two players come up, reverse the chase.

6.   The opposite team will get a point if their team member drops the object, gets tagged, or fails to walk with the directed feeling. If a player who is being chased is successful in reaching a predetermined area before they get tagged, they win a point for their team or you can let the chase last a certain amount of seconds.

7.   The winner has the most points after all teammates have had a turn.

VARIATION

The team member could tag other team members to take his/her place in the chase when the other team member is getting too close. A timer can be used to establish the time for the chase.

FOLLOW-UP

Discuss the following with your students:
- Which feeling did you like displaying the most?
- Which feeling do you display the most?

Take a Walk Feeling Directions

an angry walk

a sad walk

a tired walk

a frightened walk

a happy walk

a walk to the dentist to have a tooth pulled

a walk to a ball game

a walk after your teacher has told you how nicely you worked this morning

a walk to go home to do homework after the teacher has assigned twice as much homework as usual

a walk to take a test

a walk to the playground for extra playtime

a walk to a scary movie

a walk to church

a walk to an exciting television show

a walk to the front of the class to give a report

a walk with an older person to help them

Section IX:

Students who have been diagnosed with attention deficit disorders can practice and perfect may specific skills to assist them with their ADD. These skills may be helpful with those who have symptoms, but have not been formally diagnosed with the disorder, as well. These students need to practice specific skills in order to succeed in dealing with their impulsiveness, impatience, anxiety, inability to focus, and high levels of frustration.

The activities in this section will focus on strategies to combat these problems. Activities often incorporate the use of timers and quick movements in a game format in order to provide a high interest level while also teaching very important social and academic skills. Problem solving and decision making is also emphasized when working with these children in order to help them restructure their impulsive behaviors. Attention Deficit Disorders require multi-modal intervention approaches. These activities are an essential educational component of this approach.

ATTENTION DEFICIT DISORDERS

MIND YOUR OWN BUSINESS

Grade Levels: 1-5

Time: 30 Minutes

PURPOSE
To help students focus.

MATERIALS NEEDED
Mind Your Own Business Activity Cards
(reproduced & cutout)
Paper markers
A bag of unusual things
Dice
Paper
Pencil

OBJECT
To concentrate on the task on the
Mind Your Own Business Card and
not let anyone distract your attention.

PROCEDURES
This game is most appropriate for a small group.

1. Give each student three markers.

2. Ask each student to roll the dice. The person who rolls the highest number plays from the activity bag, all the others do a Mind You Own Business Activity on a card. The activity bag contains small unusual toys or objects. The Mind Your Own Business Activity Cards contain paper and pencil activities. For example, students may be asked to write their ABC's. All students will work on the same Mind Your Own Business Activity Card at the same time.

3. The student who rolls the highest number has the activity bag and tries to distract the others while they're doing a Mind Your Own Business Activity Card. The distracting student should be a short distance from the others. This person uses the items in the bag to try to get the other students to look up from their task. He/she may talk and make enticing comments about what he/she is doing.

4. The students doing the Mind Your Own Business Activity Card continue to do the same card while the distracting student plays with the activity bag items. The students trying to concentrate continue to focus on the activity and do not look up. They may keep repeating the same activity until time is called. Gradually increase the time.

5. If students are able to keep concentrating on the Mind Your Own Business Activity Card work, they keep their markers. If a student looks up from the card activity, the student with the bag gets one of that student's markers.

6. The winner is the one with the most markers left.

7. Continue the game by having other students take turns being the distracting student with other Mind Your Own Business Cards being acted out.

FOLLOW-UP

Discuss the following with your students:
- How did you feel when you were doing the activity card?
- What made it difficult for you to concentrate?
- What was easy for you when your were trying to concentrate?
- When you were distracting others, what were you thinking about?

Mind Your Own Business Activity Cards

Mind Your Own Business Activity Cards

Write the alphabet - upper and lower case.

Mind Your Own Business Activity Cards

Fold a paper in half four times, and put a letter in each box.

Mind Your Own Business Activity Cards

Put these in alphabetical order:

fun   girl

apple   boy

Mind Your Own Business Activity Cards

Draw a picture of a house, a tree, and a car.

Mind Your Own Business Activity Cards

Write down the numbers 1-10 with a letter beside each number.

Mind Your Own Business Activity Cards

Write your whole name five times.

Mind Your Own Business Activity Cards

Write your numbers 1-100 or as far as you can go.

Mind Your Own Business Activity Cards

Make 20 Circles.

© 1997 by YouthLight, Inc.

Mind Your Own Business Activity Cards

Write as many words as you can spell correctly.

Mind Your Own Business Activity Cards

Write as many number words as you can.

Mind Your Own Business Activity Cards

Draw five squares and put circles in each one.

Mind Your Own Business Activity Cards

Write words that begin with b.

Mind Your Own Business Activity Cards

Draw a picture of your family.

Mind Your Own Business Activity Cards

Write your friends' names down.

Mind Your Own Business Activity Cards

Write down the names of all the holidays you can think of.

Mind Your Own Business Activity Cards

Draw a picture of your room.

ONE-TRACK MIND

Grade Levels: 2-5   **Time: 30 Minutes**

PURPOSE
To teach students the skills of concentrating.

MATERIALS NEEDED

Puzzles
Paper
Pencil
Books
Index cards

OBJECT

To concentrate on the task at hand
at each of six stations and not let
the leader distract you.

PROCEDURES

This activity works best with a small group (six or less students).

1.   Introduce several activities to a group of students. (For example: reading books, playing with puzzles, drawing a picture, etc.)

2.   Place activities in different sections of the room with specific directions at each section. Sections include the following:

   a.   Put together the puzzle. Write your name on your card at #1. Take the puzzle apart.

   b.   Read three pages of this book. Write down a character in the book by #2 on your card.

   c.   Draw a picture of a sun, one flower, and a house. Take this picture with you.

   d.   Take a piece of paper and do the following:

1. Put a dot in the center.
2. Put a square around the dot.
3. Draw a small triangle at the top of the page in the center.
4. Write your name at the bottom of the page.
5. Fold the paper in half from top to bottom.
6. Take this with you.

e. Put your head down and count to 20 to yourself. Write 20 by #5 on your card.

f. Put together these blocks. All blocks must be connected. If you are able to do this, write yes on your paper by #6. Disconnect the blocks.

3. Ask six students to rotate to these sections. Set a timer or use a signal to indicate when students rotate. Establish the rotation pattern of the students in advance.

4. Tell students that you will be trying to distract them by talking to them, getting them to stop doing their activity, etc. If they pay attention to you, you are awarded a point. If they do not pay attention to you, they are awarded a point and indicate their point on their card.

5. Tally the points. If the students earn the predetermined number of points, they are winners.

FOLLOW-UP

Discuss the meaning of self-control and concentration.

Ask the children to brainstorm the "do's and don'ts" of making sure a person can concentrate in the following situations:

- Taking a test
- Studying at home
- Driving in a race
- Performing surgery on a patient
- Climbing a tall mountain

BEAT THE CLOCK

Grade Levels: 1-5

Time: 30 Minutes

PURPOSE

To help students who have trouble concentrating make a game out of any task by challenging themselves to try to "beat the clock."

MATERIALS NEEDED

Timer
Worksheet
Tokens

OBJECT

To get as many tokens as you can to trade in for prizes.

PROCEDURES

1. Tell the students that you will be challenging them with many activities in which they will be asked to beat the clock. For each successful attempt at beating the clock, they will be given a token. Tokens will later be traded for prizes.

2. The following activities are challenges for students to complete in one minute.
    a. Write your ABC's.
    b. Do 20 jumping jacks.
    c. Write the numbers 1-20 on your paper.
    d. Write down five objects in the room.
    e. Walk to the blackboard, sit on the chair, then sit cross-legged on the floor.
    f. Read three pages of a book.
    g. Turn around three times and hop across the room.
    h. Crawl around in a big circle.

    i.   Count the marbles in the jar.

    g.   Stack 20 blocks in a straight line.

3.   Begin the challenges one at a time, adding more if necessary. Give a token to each student upon completion of an activity. At the end of the challenges, tally the points and award prizes.

VARIATION

Challenge the class to complete the list successfully. Offer free time or another reward to the whole class for successful completion. Choose one student at a time to complete each challenge in a one minute time slot. Give the class one point for each task successfully completed in the allotted time.

FOLLOW-UP

Focus the discussion on the skills used to accomplish these goals and how they can also be used in the classroom. Ask the class about the following:

- Their feelings about "beating the clock."
- The amount and quality of work that they completed.
- Their plans for the next time they work on a task like this. Do they need the same time, more time, or less time?

ATTENTION CIRCLES

Grade Levels: 1-5

Time: 30 Minutes

PURPOSE
To help students distinguish between appropriate and inappropriate ways of getting attention.

MATERIALS NEEDED
Attention Circles
Paper
Pencils

OBJECT
To correctly answer questions on the Attention Circle by sticking a pencil through the appropriate hole.

PROCEDURES

1. Divide students into pairs.

2. Make enough Attention Circles so that each pair in your class will have one.
    a. To make Attention Circles, draw about a 12-inch diameter circle on a sheet of tagboard or poster board.
    b. Cut the circle out and punch about 12 pencil-sized holes around the circle, each about one inch from the outer rim of the circle.
    c. Randomly print an appropriate or inappropriate ways to seek attention next to each hole.
    d. For each appropriate answer, turn the circle over and draw a star around the hole.
    e. See examples on the next page.

3. Have one student hold the circle so another can read each item.

FRONT

BACK

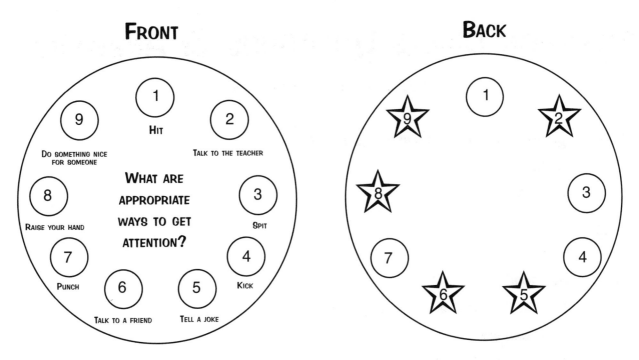

On the front circle:

- 1 — HIT
- 2 — TALK TO THE TEACHER
- 3 — SPIT
- 4 — KICK
- 5 — TELL A JOKE
- 6 — TALK TO A FRIEND
- 7 — PUNCH
- 8 — RAISE YOUR HAND
- 9 — DO SOMETHING NICE FOR SOMEONE

WHAT ARE APPROPRIATE WAYS TO GET ATTENTION?

4. Ask the student not holding the Attention Circle to stick a pencil through each hole that shows an appropriate way to seek attention. Ask the student holding the Attention Circle to watch the back side of the card and tell if the answer is correct or not. A correct answer is when the pencil comes through a star.

VARIATIONS

Use other questions and answers for the circles (see page 356).
Allow students to create other shapes.

FOLLOW-UP

Ask students to brainstorm other ideas for appropriate ways to get attention.

ATTENTION CIRCLE QUESTIONS & ANSWERS

(Circles indicate appropriate ways)

What are good ways to prepare for a test?

    ① Study

    2. Goof off

    ③ Pay attention

    ④ Memorize facts

    ⑤ Take good notes in class

    6. Stay up until 1:00 am watching movies

    ⑦ Go to bed early

    8. Eat candy for breakfast

    9. Eat peanuts during the test

What are excellent character traits?

    ① Honesty

    2. Stealing

    ③ Love

    ④ Compassion

    5. Cheating

    6. Lying

    ⑦ Helping

    ⑧ Loyalty

    ⑨ Courage

    10. Disrespect

What are ways to make new friends?

1. Spitting
2. Gossiping
3. Sharing *(circled)*
4. Helping *(circled)*
5. Stealing
6. Playing together *(circled)*
7. Giving compliments *(circled)*
8. Rolling eyes
9. Hitting
10. Talking friendly *(circled)*

What are fun things to do without taking drugs?

1. Steal a tape
2. Aggravate your mom
3. Go bowling *(circled)*
4. Go to the park *(circled)*
5. Go to the movies *(circled)*
6. Sniff glue
7. Hang out with friends *(circled)*
8. Jump on a trampoline *(circled)*
9. Try cigarettes
10. Ride a bike *(circled)*

POWER PLAY

CENTER TIME

Grade Levels: K-5   **Time: 30 Minutes**

PURPOSE

To help the class learn to follow directions and cooperate.

MATERIALS NEEDED

Books
Paper
Puzzles
Blocks
Football
Panels

OBJECT

To complete work in each activity center until instructed to move to the next without getting distracted.

PROCEDURES

1. Depending on the number of students in your group, set up an equal amount of "activity centers." For example, if you have five students, centers may be as follows:

    • Reading

    • Drawing

    • Puzzles

    • Blocks

    • Football

    You may even block off a certain area for the students to stay in. You may also use hula hoops, rope, or tape.

2. Explain to the students how each center will work, the rotation order, and the signal which will be used when it is time to change centers.

3. Using a timer, tell the students they are to do the activity until time is called. They must move quickly into the next area once the signal is given.

4. Inform them that if they become distracted from their task or do not move quickly, they will be given one point. Three points will put them out of the game.

5. If the students are fairly good at doing this, you may want to try to distract them as each student visits the centers.

FOLLOW-UP

1. Have the students discuss what they did to help them complete the tasks and ignore distractions.

2. Lead a discussion about cooperation, self-control and concentration, and how they were important factors in completing this task.

3. Have students explore ways they can use these skills during different times at school.

WAIT A MINUTE

Grade Levels: K-5

Time: 30 Minutes

PURPOSE

To help students learn to wait his/her turn.

MATERIALS NEEDED

Wait a Minute Cards (reproduced & cutout)
Button on a string
Wait a Minute Situation Cards
Wait a Minute Activity Cards

OBJECT

To correctly guess who has the button.

PROCEDURES

1. Stack the Wait a Minute Situation Cards, and Wait a Minute Activity Cards in a separate piles.

2. Choose a student to be "It" and instruct them to stand in the middle of a circle. Ask the other students to pass a button around secretly. The ones who don't have the button can pretend to pass the button by closing their hands and making it look as if the button is being passed.

3. The student who is "It" may offer three guesses as to who has the button.

4. If the person who is "It" does not guess correctly, he/she must take a Wait a Minute Situation Card (marked "S"), and a Wait a Minute Activity Card (marked "A").

5. If the student who is "It" correctly identifies the student with the button, he/she must take a situation card and an activity card instead of the person who is "It."

6. If the student doing the situation card and the activity card does the activity for one minute, he/she may choose the next person to be "It." Increase the time to two or three minutes as appropriate for age level.

7. These activities need to be done silently by the student who is "It." The other students may also practice the activity silently as it is being timed.

FOLLOW-UP

Discuss the following with your students:
- How did you feel while you were waiting a minute?
- Was it difficult or easy for you to wait a minute? Why?
- Which activity helped you to wait a minute?

WAIT A MINUTE SITUATION CARDS - S

© 1997 by YouthLight, Inc.

Wait a Minute Situation Cards - S

It is someone
else's turn.

S

Wait a Minute Situation Cards - S

The teacher is handing
out prizes.

S

Wait a Minute Situation Cards - S

The show hasn't
started.

S

Wait a Minute Situation Cards - S

You are in a
check-out line.

S

Wait a Minute Situation Cards - S

Your mom is
on the phone.

S

Wait a Minute Situation Cards - S

You're in line to
get a drink.

S

Wait a Minute Situation Cards - S

Your teacher is talking
to another teacher.

S

Wait a Minute Situation Cards - S

Your hand is up to
answer a question.

S

Wait a Minute Situation Cards - S

Another student is talking to the teacher.

S

Wait a Minute Situation Cards - S

You are riding in a car on a trip.

S

Wait a Minute Situation Cards - S

You're in the lunch line waiting.

S

Wait a Minute Situation Cards - S

You need to use a phone and someone else has it.

S

Wait a Minute Situation Cards - S

The principal comes into the classroom.

S

Wait a Minute Situation Cards - S

You're watching a program and must wait until it is over.

S

Wait a Minute Situation Cards - S

Your mom is talking to her friend.

S

Wait a Minute Situation Cards - S

You want to talk to an adult.

S

WAIT A MINUTE ACTIVITY CARDS - A

Wait a Minute Activity Cards - A **Think of as many words as you can that start with B.** **A**	**Wait a Minute Activity Cards - A** **Name as many words for "happy" as you can.** **A**
Wait a Minute Activity Cards - A **Name a food that starts with each letter of the alphabet.** **A**	**Wait a Minute Activity Cards - A** **Count by 5's as far as you can go.** **A**
Wait a Minute Activity Cards - A **Name as many different kinds of candy bars as you can.** **A**	**Wait a Minute Activity Cards - A** **Count by 1's as far as you can go.** **A**
Wait a Minute Activity Cards - A **Name the nine planets.** **A**	**Wait a Minute Activity Cards - A** **Play statues (don't move).** **A**

Wait a Minute Activity Cards - A

**Name as many kinds
of birds, and snakes,
as you can.**

A

Wait a Minute Activity Cards - A

**Say your ABC's
backwards.**

A

Wait a Minute Activity Cards - A

**Hum to yourself, "Row,
Row, Row Your Boat."**

A

Wait a Minute Activity Cards - A

**Count backwards
from 100.**

A

Wait a Minute Activity Cards - A

**Give a big grin
and freeze.**

A

Wait a Minute Activity Cards - A

**Think of the names of
the seven dwarfs.**

A

Wait a Minute Activity Cards - A

**Pinch your ear lightly
100 times.**

A

Wait a Minute Activity Cards - A

**Think of the names
of as many states
as you can.**

A

Wait a Minute Activity Cards - A

Tell yourself the story of "The Three Little Bears."

A

Wait a Minute Activity Cards - A

Say a nursery rhyme to yourself.

A

BUDDY SYSTEM

Grade Levels: K-5

Time: On going

PURPOSE

To provide more guidance and a checking system for students with study and organizational problems.

MATERIALS NEEDED

None

OBJECT

To provide a system of helping students to complete work in a timely manner by making it into a game.

PROCEDURES

1. Choose a capable, organized student to serve as a role model or "Buddy" to sit close to the student who has organizational problems.

2. Ask the Buddy to check to see if the student's homework assignments have been written down correctly also to answer quick questions on directions during classroom assignments for the student being helped.

3. Ask the Buddy to use the "Beat the Clock" method or other motivational method to encourage the other student.

4. The student being helped could also use a chart system like the one below to make a game out of learning.

1	2	3	⭐4	5	6	7
8	9	10	11	12	13	⭐14
15	16	17	18	19	20	21
22	23	⭐24	25	26	27	28
29	30	31	32	33	⭐34	35
36	37	38	39	40	41	42
43	⭐44	45	46	47	48	49

For each correct answer, for a task completed in good time, or for the student being on task, the Buddy crosses out a number in order. Whenever the student reaches a number with a star around it, he/she receives a small treat or is allowed to do a desirable activity for a short amount of time.

FOLLOW-UP

Discuss the following with your students:
- How do you feel about the Buddy System?
- How does this system help students get their work completed?

THE CIRCLE CHALLENGE

Grade Levels: K-5

Time: On going

PURPOSE

To lessen the feelings of being overwhelmed or stressed for a student doing school assignments.

MATERIALS NEEDED

Paper

Pencil

Activity sheet from which a subject the student is having problems

OBJECT

To complete the number of items in the circle at the top of the page.

PROCEDURES

1. Ask the student to draw a circle at the top of his/her assignment sheet.

2. Ask the student to decide how many items on the assignment sheet he/she can complete.

3. Instruct him/her to place that number into the circle.

4. Ask the student to work to accomplish the goal he/she set to complete the number of items in the circle.

FOLLOW-UP

Discuss the following with your students:

- How did you feel when you accomplished your circle goal?
- Do you think you could do any more items?

Section X:

SAFETY

The safety of young children is in question in every setting. As educators, we need to increase students' awareness of potentially dangerous situations in order to strengthen their abilities to successfully respond in these situations to protect themselves and others.

The activities in this section examine specific situations and reinforce the concept of staying away from dangerous situations through increased awareness and smart thinking. Students must be taught to view every unfamiliar situation as potentially dangerous and to take appropriate precautions for self-protection. Running away and talking to adults they know and trust are two strategies of utmost importance. The activities examine these strategies and provide an outlet through which professionals can once again emphasize child protection and safety.

THE THREE LITTLE PIGS

Grade Levels: K-5

Time: 30 Minutes

PURPOSES

To increase students' awareness of personal safety issues.
To practice awareness of these safety issues.

MATERIALS NEEDED

The Three Little Pigs adapted review
The Three Little Pigs Situation Cards
(reproduced & cutout)

OBJECT

To earn points by ringing a bell first
before the wolf gets it.

PROCEDURES

1. Review the story of "The Three Little Pigs." Emphasize how the wolf approached the pigs and tried tricking them in order to catch them.

2. Ask for two student volunteers for each scenario. Instruct one student to take a card labeled "Wolf" and one student to take a card labeled "Pig." The players must keep it a secret who they are.

3. Instruct the two students to stand facing each other with a small bell between them on a chair, a desk, or a stool.

4. Read either from a wolf or a friendly pig statement. (see pages 378-381).

5. Based upon the card they draw, if either the pig or the wolf feels threatened, he/she will grab the bell. A point is earned for the student who gets the bell. Disclose which student was the wolf team or the pig team after the bell is grabbed. Hopefully, the pig team will be more alert and win. Students may play more than once and serve as a different character, the whole class is pulling for the pig to win.

6. If the statement is not threatening and the bell is grabbed anyway, that student loses a point.

FOLLOW-UP

Discuss the following with your students:

- Do you feel more alert to danger now? Why?
- How do you feel when you're alert to danger?
- How can this practice game help you be more self-protective?
- What did you learn about being safe that you weren't aware of before?

Adapted Review of The Three Little Pigs

Once upon a time, as you remember, there were three little pigs who each built a house. However, a wicked wolf destroyed two of the pig's houses even though the first two little pigs were careful not to allow the wolf in their houses.

The most important part of the story was when the wolf tried to trick the third little pig. As you remember, the third little pig always outsmarted the wolf by planning ahead and by recognizing that the wolf was very dangerous, even though the wolf talked in a friendly manner.

The wolf tried to trick the third little pig by enticing him to go pick apples, an activity the little pig really enjoyed. The wolf also tried to trick the third little pig to go to the fair which sounded like a lot of fun. In each of these situations, the little pig made sure to keep a safe distance between himself and the wolf. The wolf was outsmarted in the end by being tricked by the pig.

THE GINGERBREAD MAN

Grade Levels: 1-5

Time: 30 Minutes

PURPOSE

To help students practice being assertive during self protection situations.

MATERIALS NEEDED

The Gingerbread Man adapted review
The Three Little Pigs & The Gingerbread Man
Situation Cards (reproduced & cutout)

OBJECT

To call out, "Run, run, run" first if a
dangerous situation card is read aloud.

PROCEDURES

1. Review the adapted story of "The Gingerbread Man." Emphasize how the Gingerbread Man protected himself from everyone trying to get him, from the old woman, the old man, the farmer, the cow, etc. Explain what happened when he let his guard down with the tricky fox.

2. This game is similar to "Locomotive" or "Round the World." Choose a student to be the Gingerbread Man and instruct him/her to stand behind a student seated at a desk.

3. Read a Gingerbread Man Situation Card (see pages 378-381.) If the situation card calls for the Gingerbread Man to be assertive and protect himself, he or she must call out, "Run, run, run" first. (The Gingerbread Man in the story said, "Run, run, run, as fast as you can. You can't catch me, I'm the Gingerbread Man.") If the situation does not call for the Gingerbread Man to be assertive or to protect himself, he/she remains silent.

4. The seated student gets to be the next Gingerbread Man if he/she calls out, "I got you," before the Gingerbread Man can say "Run, run, run." The student must call out if a dangerous situation card is read.

5. If the standing student calls out first, the Gingerbread Man must move to the next student's desk and continue the contest of who can call out first.

6. The Gingerbread Man, who gets all the way around the room or safely past five people, wins. Then a new Gingerbread Man is chosen.

VARIATION

When the Gingerbread Man wins by being first to call out, he/she must follow, "Run, run, run," with an assertive statement that could be applied to the situation.

FOLLOW-UP

Discuss the following with your students:

- How did you feel when you were assertive as a Gingerbread Man?
- What helped you to realize that the situation needed for you to be assertive?

Adapted Review of The Gingerbread Man

Once upon a time, as you remember, a little old man and little old woman baked a Gingerbread Man. But as they opened the oven door, the Gingerbread Man jumped out and ran away calling, "Run, run, run, as fast as you can. You can't catch me, I'm the Gingerbread Man."

The little Gingerbread Man ran away from several dangerous situations with the pig, the cow, and the field full of threshers. He very wisely saw the danger present so he avoided slowing down. He did, however, get too self-confident and lose his watchfulness when the fox made a deal with him to take him across the river, The fox had tricked him, and when the Gingerbread Man could no longer run to safety, the fox said, "I got you."

THREE LITTLE PIGS & THE GINGERBREAD MAN SITUATION CARDS

MIX THE FRIENDLY PIG AND WOLF STATEMENTS TOGETHER INTO ONE STACK OF CARDS.

FRIENDLY PIG:

Three Little Pig (Friendly Pig) & Gingerbread Man Situation Cards THE TEACHER SAYS, "HELLO LITTLE BOY/GIRL." 	Three Little Pig (Friendly Pig) & Gingerbread Man Situation Cards YOUR FRIEND SAYS, "HAVE A NICE DAY."
Three Little Pig (Friendly Pig) & Gingerbread Man Situation Cards THE COUNSELOR SAYS, "YOU LOOK PRETTY/HANDSOME IN THAT OUTFIT." 	Three Little Pig (Friendly Pig) & Gingerbread Man Situation Cards THE PRINCIPAL SAYS, "IT LOOKS LIKE A PRETTY DAY."
Three Little Pig (Friendly Pig) & Gingerbread Man Situation Cards YOUR BEST FRIEND SAYS, "GOOD TO SEE YOU." 	Three Little Pig (Friendly Pig) & Gingerbread Man Situation Cards YOUR UNCLE ASKS, "WHAT GRADE ARE YOU IN?"

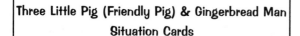

Three Little Pig (Friendly Pig) & Gingerbread Man
Situation Cards

YOUR TEACHER ASKS,
"HOW ARE YOU?"

Three Little Pig (Friendly Pig) & Gingerbread Man
Situation Cards

YOUR NEIGHBOR ASKS,
"DO YOU LIKE SCHOOL?"

Three Little Pig (Friendly Pig) & Gingerbread Man
Situation Cards

YOU DAD SAYS,
"WHAT A PRETTY/HANDSOME LITTLE BOY/GIRL YOU ARE."

Three Little Pig (Friendly Pig) & Gingerbread Man
Situation Cards

YOUR FRIEND'S MOM ASKS,
"ARE YOU HAVING A GOOD TIME?"

WOLF:

Three Little Pig (Wolf) & Gingerbread Man
Situation Cards

SOMEONE UNFAMILIAR PATS YOU ON THE SHOULDER, HEAD, ETC.

Three Little Pig (Wolf) & Gingerbread Man
Situation Cards

SOMEONE SAYS, "CAN YOU HELP ME MAIL SOME LETTERS OR CARRY THIS TO THE CAR?"

Three Little Pig (Wolf) & Gingerbread Man
Situation Cards

SOMEONE AT THE STORE ASKS,
"WHAT'S YOUR NAME?"

Three Little Pig (Wolf) & Gingerbread Man
Situation Cards

SOMEONE UNFAMILIAR SAYS,
"YOUR MOM IS GOING TO BE LATE AND WANTS ME TO PICK YOU UP."

Three Little Pig (Wolf) & Gingerbread Man
Situation Cards

 SOMEONE AT THE MALL ASKS:
"WHERE DO YOU LIVE?"

Three Little Pig (Wolf) & Gingerbread Man
Situation Cards

A STRANGER ON THE
PLAYGROUND SAYS,
"I'VE GOT A GIFT
FOR YOU."

Three Little Pig (Wolf) & Gingerbread Man
Situation Cards

 SOMEONE DELIVERING A
PACKAGE SAYS,
"I KNOW YOUR MOM.
I WORK WITH HER."

Three Little Pig (Wolf) & Gingerbread Man
Situation Cards

SOMEONE UNFAMILIAR SAYS,
"LET ME GIVE YOU
TEN DOLLARS."

Three Little Pig (Wolf) & Gingerbread Man
Situation Cards

SOMEONE UNFAMILIAR SAYS,
"YOUR MOM HAS BEEN IN A TERRIBLE
ACCIDENT. LET ME TAKE
YOU TO SEE HER."

Three Little Pig (Wolf) & Gingerbread Man
Situation Cards

SOMEONE UNFAMILIAR SAYS,
"IF YOU HELP ME CARRY
SOME BOXES, I'LL GIVE
YOU TWENTY DOLLARS.

Three Little Pig (Wolf) & Gingerbread Man
Situation Cards

SOMEONE IN THE PARK SAYS, "I'VE GOT
A GREAT MOTORCYCLE TO RIDE ON.
WOULD YOU LIKE
A RIDE?"

Three Little Pig (Wolf) & Gingerbread Man
Situation Cards

A MAN IN THE STORE SAYS,
"I'VE GOT A GREAT NEW TOY
TO GIVE YOU FREE."

Page 381

Three Little Pig (Wolf) & Gingerbread Man Situation Cards

A TEENAGER AT THE TRACK SAYS, "LET'S GO FLY THIS PRETTY KITE."

Three Little Pig (Wolf) & Gingerbread Man Situation Cards

A MAN IN A LONG COAT SAYS, "LET ME TAKE YOUR PICTURE."

Three Little Pig (Wolf) & Gingerbread Man Situation Cards

A STRANGER AT YOUR DOOR SAYS, "OPEN THE DOOR RIGHT NOW OR YOU'RE IN TROUBLE."

Three Little Pig (Wolf) & Gingerbread Man Situation Cards

A STRANGER AT THE STORE SAYS, "I'VE GOT SOME GOOD CANDY TO GIVE TO YOU FREE."

Three Little Pig (Wolf) & Gingerbread Man Situation Cards

A CALLER ASKS, "IS YOUR MOM/DAD AT HOME?"

Three Little Pig (Wolf) & Gingerbread Man Situation Cards

THE BUS DRIVER SAYS, "I'VE GOT SOME FREE TICKETS TO GIVE TO YOU FOR THE AMUSEMENT PARK."

Three Little Pig (Wolf) & Gingerbread Man Situation Cards

A STRANGER SAYS, "I'M GOING TO MAKE YOU A MOVIE STAR. COME WITH ME."

Three Little Pig (Wolf) & Gingerbread Man Situation Cards

A MAN IN A BLUE CAR SAYS, "YOU STOLE A BICYCLE AND YOU'RE IN TROUBLE. GIVE ME YOUR NAME AND ADDRESS."

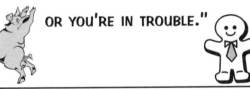